LEBANON

LEBANON

WILLIAM E. SHAPIRO

A GROLIER COMPANY

Franklin Watts
New York/London/Toronto/Sydney/1984
An Impact Book

Photographs courtesy of
UPI: pp. 6, 37, 42, 45, 53, 63;
AP/Wide World: pp. 9, 15, 20, 54

Map courtesy of Vantage Art, Inc.

Library of Congress Cataloging in Publication Data

Shapiro, William E.
Lebanon.

(An Impact book)
Bibliography: p.
Includes index.
Summary: Explores the conflict in war-torn Lebanon,
giving a history of the land, the people, the politics,
and the ethnic problems.
1. Lebanon—History—1975-   —Juvenile literature.
[1. Lebanon—History]   I. Title.
DS87.S484 1984   956.92'044   84-11828
ISBN 0-531-04854-3

CONTENTS

LEBANON

CHAPTER 1

THE LEBANESE TRAGEDY

Lebanon, a nation that once proudly called itself the Switzerland of the Middle East, is today a country in name only. Its government controls little more than half of the nation's capital, Beirut. Its once-vibrant economy is a shambles. And its society is fragmented—so fragmented, some believe, that it may be impossible to re-create a unified state responsive to the needs of all its varied peoples.

For nearly a decade this hapless nation has suffered continuous civil war among its various religious and ethnic groups. It has been invaded twice by Israel, which now controls all of southern Lebanon, and it has been occupied by Syria, which controls most of eastern and northern Lebanon. Nearly 500,000 Palestinians—refugees from the Arab-Israeli wars—live in Lebanon, where they have formed a "state within a state." And a succession of peacekeeping forces—Arab, United Nations, and Western—have not only failed to establish peace, but have exacerbated the already horrific situation.

Why is this once-prosperous nation on the verge of total collapse? There are a number of reasons, but the primary one is that the Lebanese people belong to at least fifteen different religious sects and their loyalty to these sects is greater than their loyalty to a united Lebanon. Had the people's sense of nationhood been stronger, they would not have suffered the destruction of the past decade.

Why haven't the Lebanese people been able to put aside their sectarian differences and work toward a stable government that represents all of the people? The complete answer to this question lies deep within the unique history of Lebanon, which will be detailed in Chapter 3. But—for the purpose of this introductory overview—we need go back only to 1943, the year that France, which ruled Lebanon as a League of Nations mandate, reluctantly gave the nation its independence. As independence approached, the nation's two most populous and powerful sects, the Maronite Christians and the Sunni Moslems, formulated what is known as the National Pact—an unwritten agreement that spelled out the country's political makeup as well as its general orientation in foreign affairs.

The National Pact allocated political power to Lebanon's religious sects on the basis of population. The most recent census had been held in 1932, and it placed the number of Christians at slightly more than 50 percent of the population. As a result, it was agreed that the president of Lebanon would always be a Maronite Christian and the prime minister would always be a Sunni Moslem. Other important positions were given to other sects. The president of the Chamber of Deputies, for example, would always be a Shiite Moslem and the defense minister would be a Druse. In addition, the Christians were to have six seats in Parliament for every five seats held by Moslems. This system guaranteed the Maronite Christians control of Lebanon.

The National Pact enabled the country to make a relatively smooth transition from mandate to independent state, but it also entrenched the long-standing Lebanese practice of allocating political power along religious, or confessional, lines. So

Lebanon, for the first time in its history, became an independent nation with a central government, yet the people continued to give their loyalty and support to their own sects rather than to the national government. More ominously, each sect maintained a militia even though there was a national army.

This system worked well enough for fifteen years. From 1943 until 1958 the nation's economy boomed and Beirut was transformed into the showcase city of the Mediterranean. The government seemed stable enough, but there were problems boiling beneath the surface and in the mid-1950s the system began to come apart. For one thing, the Moslems, especially the poorer Shiites, had a substantially higher birthrate than the Christians; many people believed that the Shiites had surpassed the Maronites in population. But the Christians would not allow a new census to be taken, for this would have meant a reallocation of the nation's political power, with the Moslem sects gaining at the expense of the Christians. With their hopes for political gains dampened, the Shiites became disenchanted.

Another problem with Lebanon of the 1940s and 1950s was the fact that the economic boom was not enjoyed by all. Once again, the Maronites and other Christians benefited most. The Sunnis garnered some part of the nation's newfound wealth, but the Shiites remained at the bottom of the economic ladder.

Perhaps these political and economic problems could have been resolved by the Lebanese people. Perhaps not. But beginning in the late 1940s, a new and disturbing dimension was added to the conflict between the Christians and the Moslems: the arrival of hundreds of thousands of Palestinian refugees. These refugees had fled from Palestine during the 1948 Arab-Israeli War that accompanied the birth of the state of Israel. They settled in southern Lebanon as well as in and around Beirut. Most of them were Moslems, and they supported their Lebanese coreligionists in their demand for greater political power and economic rewards.

The National Pact did not deal solely with internal Lebanese political power. It also established some broad guidelines for the future conduct of the nation's foreign policy. These guidelines, a well-meant compromise between the Maronites and Sunnis, were designed to reassure Moslems and Christians alike that Lebanon was a country for all peoples. For example, the ruling Maronites, despite their generally Western outlook and their strong ties to France, accepted the fact that Lebanon was an Arab country and, as such, a part of the Arab world. The Moslems, in turn, agreed not to espouse Pan-Arab unity and not to attempt to bring about a merger with neighboring Syria.

This part of the National Pact began to unravel very early on. In 1949, the Syrian National party, which espoused a merger with Syria, tried to overthrow the regime of the Maronite president, Bishara Khury, who had helped devise the National Pact. Just three years later, in Egypt, Gamal Abdel Nasser overthrew the conservative and oppressive government of King Farouk and began advocating a militant form of Pan-Arabism. Nasser's beliefs—including his strong anti-Western philosophy—appealed to many Moslems in Lebanon, but they frightened the Maronites, who feared that they would be "drowned in a sea of Islam."

The Maronites' fears prompted them to draw closer to the West, especially the United States. In 1957 Camille Chamoun, who had become president in 1952, accepted the so-called Eisenhower Doctrine, which pledged the United States to come to the aid of "any nation or group of nations requesting assistance against armed aggression from any country controlled by international communism."

In 1958, Chamoun tried to force Parliament to change the Lebanese constitution so that he could serve a second term as president. His actions were responsible for Lebanon's first civil war. His opponents were primarily Sunnis, but many Shiites and even some Christians opposed Chamoun's illegal attempt to serve a second term. When the fighting spread, the Lebanese army refused to fire on the rebels. As a result—even though the conflict was an internal one—Chamoun blamed the revolt on

"Communists and Nasserites" and called on the United States to honor the terms of the Eisenhower Doctrine. Earlier Egypt and Syria, two countries which at the time were heavily armed by the Soviet Union, had merged to form the United Arab Republic; and on July 14, 1958, the pro-Western government of Iraq was overthrown. With the Lebanese government fearful of the Pan-Arabism implicit in the Egypt-Syria merger and the United States increasingly concerned about Soviet inroads in the Middle East, President Dwight Eisenhower ordered U.S. Marines into Lebanon. They landed on July 15. Predictably, the Soviet Union denounced the move.

Lebanon, with troubles enough from its warring sects and from the presence of hundreds of thousands of Palestinian refugees, was now thrust into the middle of the East-West conflict.

The 1958 civil war was brief. Chamoun finally agreed to step down when his term as president expired in September; the Moslem rebels then ended the fighting. The U.S. Marines—they never fired a shot—were soon withdrawn. But the civil war had far-reaching effects. From this point on the Moslems of Lebanon would increase their demands for closer ties with other Arab states; and the Christians, especially the Maronites, would look increasingly for support from the West and from Israel. The National Pact was well on its way to becoming meaningless.

Throughout the 1960s, the Christians and the Moslems became more and more inflexible in their attitudes toward each other. Around the time of the 1967 Arab-Israeli War, yet another troubling dimension was added to the worsening internal situation. Palestinian guerrillas were now raiding Israel from Lebanese territory—and the Israeli government held the Lebanese government responsible. Yet the Lebanese army was too weak to curb the Palestinians; and it was certainly incapable of protecting its own territory during Israeli reprisal raids.

This situation worsened dramatically after 1970, when the Palestinian guerrillas in Jordan were ousted by troops loyal to

*In the 1950s thousands of Palestinian
refugees fled to Lebanon where they lived
in camps such as this one near Tripoli.*

King Hussein. The guerrillas—many of them with their families—joined their companions in Lebanon, which was now the only country that allowed—or at least could not prevent—Palestinian raids against Israel. Thus, Lebanon increasingly became the focus of attention for both Israel and its Arab neighbors. Inevitably, these countries became involved in Lebanon's internal affairs. So, too, did the Palestinians.

By the early 1970s, the Palestine Liberation Organization (PLO), which the Arab governments recognized in 1974 as the "sole, legitimate representative of the Palestinian people," controlled not only the Moslem areas of Beirut, but most of southern Lebanon and the Bekaa Valley. The Palestinians had many allies among the Sunnis and various leftist groups. They trained and armed radical groups that opposed the Christian-dominated Lebanese government. The only major Moslem group to oppose the Palestinians were the Shiites of southern Lebanon, because it was their homes, villages, and farms that were destroyed when the Israelis conducted their reprisal raids. By 1975 these raids had caused massive destruction in southern Lebanon. Tens of thousands of Shiites had been forced to flee north, especially to Beirut.

As the situation worsened in 1975, Pierre Gemayel, the leader of the Phalange party, the dominant Maronite Christian political group, demanded that the Palestinians be ousted from Lebanon. However, many Moslems demanded that the Lebanese government put a halt to the Israeli reprisal raids. The Moslems also increased their demands for a fair share of the nation's wealth. With the pressure mounting, another civil war was all but inevitable.

The civil war that began in 1975 is sometimes described as a Christian-Moslem civil war, but this description is not entirely accurate. It was really a war of Rightists against Leftists, of politically and socially conservative groups against the poor and socialist-oriented segments of Lebanese society. Many poorer Christians who resented the power and wealth of the Maronites allied themselves with the Moslems, and many middle-class Moslems with a stake in maintaining the status quo allied themselves with the Maronites.

The civil war quickly escalated to include the PLO, whose well-trained and heavily armed guerrillas fought alongside the Leftists. Once the PLO joined the fray, it was just a matter of time before the conflict became internationalized. The Maronites were supported primarily by the United States and Israel. The PLO and its allies were supported by Syria and Libya, both of whom received military equipment from the Soviet Union. Syria, however, would soon change sides.

By the middle of 1976, the Leftist alliance was on the verge of defeating the Lebanese army and the Christian militias— the military wings of the various Christian groups and political parties. Syria opposed a complete Leftist victory for two reasons. First, it feared that a Leftist victory, which meant a PLO victory, would bring about an Israeli invasion of Lebanon. Second, Syria preferred a stalemate in the situation, for this would have increased Syria's ability to dominate Lebanese internal affairs. A victorious Left would not have needed Syrian help in dealing with the Christians.

To prevent the Leftist victory, Syria devised a plan to end the civil war and, at the same time, give increased political power to the predominantly Moslem Leftists. But the Leftists, sensing that military victory was near, rejected Syria's plan. Syrian President Hafez al-Assad then ordered some 30,000 Syrian troops into Lebanon to aid the Christians. The tide of the war soon turned, and the Lebanese Christian militias together with Syrian forces recaptured most of the territory that had been taken by the PLO and its Leftist allies. A ceasefire was arranged in October.

The destruction in Lebanon, after a year and a half of fighting, was staggering. At least 40,000 people were dead. The economy was in ruins. Entire villages were destroyed. Thousands of middle-class Lebanese, especially Christians, were fleeing the country. The viciousness exhibited by both sides— including massacres and rape—resulted in hatreds so deep that Lebanon, many observers fear, may never again be a country in which the two dominant religious groups could cooperate effectively for any lengthy period of time.

This photograph shows two genera-
tions of Maronite Christian leaders.
Lebanon's president, Amin Gemayel
(left), is speaking at a meeting
at the Military Academy in
Beirut. In the center is his father,
Pierre Gemayel, the leader of the
Phalangist Party, and at the far right
is Camille Chamoun, a former
president of Lebanon.

Although a cease-fire was arranged in October 1976, the civil war of 1975–1976 never really ended; the fighting and destruction continued into the 1980s.

Syria, which regards the Bekaa Valley as vital to its security, kept its troops in Lebanon. The PLO, which still has as its goal the destruction of the state of Israel, once again began to raid Israeli territory from southern Lebanon. And Israel, in retaliation, invaded Lebanon in 1978 and set up a zone in the southern part of the country that was controlled by a Christian militia that took its orders from the Israeli army command. If the Bekaa Valley was vital to Syrian security, southern Lebanon was vital to Israeli security.

The Israeli troops withdrew under very strong international pressure, but in 1982 they returned with a vengeance. This time the Israelis destroyed the PLO presence in southern Lebanon, but they also destroyed much of southern Lebanon and then advanced to Beirut, where they forced thousands of PLO fighters to flee the country.

On May 17, 1983, the Lebanese government of Maronite Christian Amin Gemayel signed an agreement with Israel that provided for a security zone in southern Lebanon to protect Israel against PLO attacks. Syria strongly opposed this agreement and refused to move its troops out of Lebanon.

In the meantime, in the fall of 1982, American marines— as well as military units from France, Italy, and Great Britain—arrived in Lebanon. The U.S. Marines were there to help the government extend its area of control. But in the fall of 1983, after Israel withdrew its forces from the Shuf Mountains to the southeast of Beirut, fighting broke out between Christian and Druse militias for control of the area. Shiite Moslems also started battling the Christian militias and the Lebanese army. Soon the marines and American naval ships offshore were supporting the Gemayel government.

There was a brief cease-fire at the end of 1983, but in February 1984 the country exploded again. The Moslem militias dealt one defeat after another to the American-trained Lebanese soldiers and took over West Beirut. The Moslem mem-

bers of Gemayel's government resigned. The U.S. Marines—
nearly three hundred of them had been killed—were ordered
out of Lebanon and onto the warships sitting off the coast. The
British and Italian troops also withdrew, leaving only the
French forces in Beirut. Here they patrolled the "Green Line,"
the dividing line between Christian East Beirut and predominantly Moslem West Beirut. At the end of March, the French
also withdrew from Lebanon.

With American support ending, Gemayel was forced to
turn to Syria in an effort to save his government and end the
fighting. In exchange for Gemayel's abrogation of the May 17,
1983, agreement with Israel, Syria agreed to get the Druse and
Shiites to end the fighting and to meet with Gemayel in Switzerland in March to discuss the possibility of national reconciliation—including a revamping of the Lebanese political system. This meeting ended in failure. But in April Gemayel
named the pro-Syrian Rashid Karami as prime minister.
Karami immediately tried to form a government of national
unity, calling on members of all of Lebanon's major sects to
serve in the cabinet.

At this writing, the Israelis still control southern Lebanon.
The Syrians and their Druse and Shiite allies control most of
the rest of the country. Should the government of national unity bring peace to the country, Lebanon would still face a massive economic reconstruction task, for Beirut is almost a
wasteland, dozens of villages have been totally destroyed, and
tens of thousands of people have been killed and wounded.
The economy will have to be rebuilt almost from scratch.

Why has this tragedy befallen Lebanon? To gain some
insights we must search out the historical roots of the conflict
between the nation's various religious sects. But first, in the
next chapter, we will look at the land and people of this war-
torn nation.

CHAPTER 2

THE LAND AND THE PEOPLE

Lebanon lies on the eastern shore of the Mediterranean Sea, in that part of southwestern Asia known as the Middle East. Because of its location—at the crossroads of Asia, Europe, and Africa—Lebanon has been a center of commerce and trade for thousands of years. It has also been on the route of numerous conquering armies.

With an area of 4,015 square miles (10,400 sq km), Lebanon is one of the smallest countries in the Middle East. It is smaller than every state in the United States except Delaware, Rhode Island, and Connecticut. Lebanon is sandwiched between Syria in the north and east and Israel in the south. The maximum distance from the nation's northern border to its southern one is only 130 miles (210 km). And the maximum distance from the Mediterranean Sea to the Lebanon-Syria border is 50 miles (80 km). In the south, along the border with Israel, Lebanon's eastern border is only 20 miles (32 km) from the sea.

Lebanon has four distinct geographical regions: a narrow—but fertile—coastal plain; two roughly parallel mountain ranges that run the full length of the country—the Lebanon Mountains and the Anti-Lebanon Mountains; and a fertile valley—the Bekaa—that lies between the two ranges.

The narrow plain along the Mediterranean coast is the most densely populated part of Lebanon. Here and there the Lebanon Mountains push down to the sea, and thus there is no coastal plain. In other spots the plain is so narrow that there is barely enough room for a road. However, in a number of places the coastal plain is wide enough to accommodate population centers, and it is here, between the foothills of the mountains and the Mediterranean Sea, that two of Lebanon's most important cities—Beirut and Tripoli—are located.

Beirut—Lebanon's capital, largest city, and major port—is located at about the midpoint of the country's coastline. Today, much of Beirut lies in ruins. It has been a battlefield on which the contending forces have warred to see who could cause the greatest destruction. But before 1975, when the civil war erupted, Beirut was the nation's cultural and commercial heart and one of the most beautiful and prosperous cities in the Middle East.

Beirut was founded in 3000 B.C. by the Phoenicians. Before the beginning of the Christian era it was ruled in turn by the Assyrians, Babylonians, Persians, Macedonians, and Romans. The Romans called the city Berytus; it was an important administrative center of the Roman Empire. In 551 A.D., however, the city was destroyed by an earthquake and tidal waves. It was not rebuilt until the Arabs took control a century later. Following Arab rule, Beirut was controlled by the Crusaders, Egyptians, Ottoman Turks, and the French, who, in 1920, made it the capital of Lebanon, their League of Nations mandate.

Under the French and later as the capital of an independent Lebanon, the city of Beirut prospered. Ocean-going ships called at the city's protected harbor and shipping became a major industry. A busy railroad and highway linked Beirut to the interior of Lebanon and to Damascus, the capital of Syria. Because Lebanon was a relatively tranquil oasis in the turbulent Middle East, bankers and businessmen flocked to Beirut. High-rise apartment buildings, commercial buildings, and luxury hotels were built on or near the beautiful Mediterranean coast. Beirut airport, south of the city, became the busiest in the Middle East. As business boomed, Lebanese citizens flocked to the city in search of jobs and opportunities; by 1975 nearly one out of every four Lebanese lived in or near their capital city.

Beirut had art galleries and museums, as well as three universities. Its nightlife rivaled that of many European cities. Expensive shops of every kind lined the streets. But, as in the rest of the country, residential areas were divided along religious, social, and ethnic lines. Christians were dominant in one area, Moslems in another. Some areas near the city were turned into camps for the Palestinian refugees who had fled their homeland during the Arab-Israeli wars.

Beirut today is not a pretty city. Beginning with the civil war of 1975–1976, it has seen nearly a decade of death and destruction. The Moslems in West Beirut, the Christians in East Beirut, and the Druse in the hills above the city seem to be engaged in a never-ending artillery duel. Nearly 1,800 bombs and car-bombs have been set off within the city limits. Once-beautiful hotels, apartment houses, and commercial buildings are pockmarked with shell holes. Barricades are everywhere, and more and more people are lining up in front of Western embassies to get visas for other countries. By 1984, more than 200,000 Lebanese had fled the seemingly unending warfare. Beirut, a once-proud and beautiful city with a vibrant economy, is really not a single city anymore. It is, like the rest of the

Beirut as it looked from the air in 1955, before years of civil war reduced much of the once-beautiful city to rubble

country, war-torn and partitioned between Moslems and Christians.

Lebanon's second largest city, Tripoli, is also on the coast, some 40 miles (64 km) north of Beirut. Because most of the people in this city are Sunni Moslems, it had, until 1983, escaped the destruction brought to Beirut by the Moslem-Christian fighting. But in late 1983, warring factions of the Palestine Liberation Organization fought their battles in and around Tripoli. Hundreds of Lebanese were killed, buildings were destroyed, and oil-storage tanks were set ablaze. A large part of Tripoli's population fled the battle area, but returned in December 1983 after the PLO forces loyal to Yasir Arafat were evacuated.

Other important cities on the coastal plain are Juniye, Sidon, and Tyre. Sidon and Tyre are south of Beirut and have been occupied by Israeli troops since the Israeli invasion of Lebanon in 1982.

East of the coastal plain are the Lebanon Mountains, which, during more peaceful times, were a skiers' paradise. The peaks rise steeply to 10,000 feet (3,000 m) and are cut by great canyons, some of which are 1,000 feet (300 m) deep. The highest point in the mountains is Qurnat as Sawda, which rises to 10,115 feet (3,083 m). Not far from this peak is one of the few remaining groves of Lebanon cedars, some of which have been standing for perhaps a thousand years. Forests of cedar once covered these mountains, but overcutting and overgrazing by goats have left the mountain slopes almost bare.

The Lebanon Mountains are dotted with scores of small villages, some of them Christian, some Moslem, and some Druse. The economy of these villages is based on agriculture; the crops include apples, peaches, grapes, melons, beans, tomatoes, and tobacco.

East of the Lebanon Mountains is the Bekaa Valley, a fertile strip of land 110 miles (180 km) long and 6 to 10 miles (10 to 16 km) wide. Zahle, the third largest city in the country, is in the valley. The country's two most important rivers, the Litani and the Orontes, rise in the northern Bekaa near Baalbek, a city that dates to Roman times. The Litani flows southwest through the Bekaa Valley and then empties into the Mediterranean Sea north of Tyre. Its waters are used for irrigation, so it becomes a mere trickle by the time it gets to the sea. The Orontes rises not far from the Litani, but it flows northward between the Lebanon and Anti-Lebanon Mountains, wending its way into Syria.

Lebanon's eastern border with Syria is formed by the Anti-Lebanon Mountains. This mountain chain—which is not quite so high as the Lebanon Mountains—is sparsely populated. Its most striking peak is Mount Hermon, which at 9,232 feet (2,814 m) is snowcapped the entire year.

This land—the coastal plain, the two mountain ranges, and the Bekaa Valley—is home to 3,480,000 Lebanese. Almost all of the people, whether they are Christian or Moslem, are Arabs, and Lebanon is an Arab country. Most of the people can speak French or English or both, but Arabic is the national language. However, the national unity that usually comes from a common language and heritage has eluded the Lebanese people. In many ways, the country is less a nation than a collection of feudal-like baronies based on religious lines. Each religious community has its own leaders and its own fighting force, or militia. It is reminiscent of China during the early years of the twentieth century, when that nation had a weak central government and was ruled by various warlords scattered throughout the country, each seeking political and economic dominance.

The Moslems, who now constitute more than half the population, are divided into three major sects: the Shiites, the Sunnis, and the Druse. The Christians include the Maronites, Greek Orthodox, Greek Catholics, Orthodox and Catholic Armenians, and Protestants. But neither the Christians nor the Moslems are truly unified; throughout their history Moslem and Christian sects have fought for political and economic gain.

The following table shows the religious composition of Lebanon. The population figures are estimates, because no census has been taken since 1932:

Moslem Sect	Population	Percent of Population
Shiites	1,000,000	29
Sunnis	600,000	17
Druse	350,000	10
Total Moslem	1,950,000	56

Christian Sect	Population	Percent of Population
Maronites	580,000	17
Greek Orthodox	350,000	10
Greek Catholic	250,000	7
Armenian Orthodox and Catholic	250,000	7
Protestant and others	100,000	3
Total Christian	1,530,000	44

Total Christian and Moslem	3,480,000

In addition, some 500,000 Palestinians live in Lebanon; about 60,000 of them have obtained Lebanese citizenship.

*Lebanese farmers harvest potatoes
in the Bekaa Valley.*

The Moslems, who in 1932 were in the minority, now make up 56 percent of the population of Lebanon. The Shiites, the poorest of the Moslem sects, number about 1 million. They are concentrated in West Beirut and in the city's southern suburbs, as well as in southern Lebanon and in and around Baalbek in the Bekaa Valley.

The most important Shiite political party is called Amal. It is headed by Nabih Berri, who also commands the Amal militia, which numbers about 10,000 fighters. The militia is a major force in West Beirut and in the city's southern suburbs, as well as in Baalbek. Amal is allied with the Druse and they have coordinated their effort to oust the Maronite-dominated government of Amin Gemayel. The Shiites are armed by the Syrians, but they also receive some arms from Iran, whose ruler, Ayatollah Ruhollah Khomeini, is a Shiite, as are most Iranians.

The Shiites of southern Lebanon were among those who welcomed the Israeli invasion of 1982, as a means of getting rid of the Palestinian fighters who lived there, using Shiite towns and villages as jumping-off places for raids into Israel. The Palestinian guerrillas not only dominated and controlled Shiite towns, but were responsible for the Israeli reprisal raids that resulted in the destruction of Shiite homes, farms, and villages. But this peace between the Shiites and Israelis did not last long. As the Israeli rule became harsh—for security reasons, the Israelis said—many Shiites turned against them, initiating a number of terrorist attacks against Israeli forces and headquarters. Some, however, still preferred the Israelis to a return of the PLO and joined an Israeli-backed Christian militia headed by Colonel Saad Haddad, a renegade Lebanese army officer.

The Sunnis number about 600,000 and are concentrated in West Beirut, Tripoli, Sidon, and Akkar, in the northernmost part of the country. Rashid Karami, a former Lebanese prime minister, is the leader of the Sunnis in Tripoli and the most influential Sunni in the country. Karami, along with Druse leader Walid Jumblatt and Maronite Christian Suleiman Franjieh, opposed the government of Amin Gemayel, the Maronite

Christian. But in April 1984 Karami became prime minister once again.

The Sunni militia, Morbitun, a force of 5,000 well-trained fighters, is stationed in West Beirut, Tripoli, and other Sunni areas.

The Druse, a secretive Moslem sect, number about 350,000, but their influence is greater than these numbers would indicate. The Druse live primarily in the Shuf Mountains and in other areas to the south and east of Beirut. The major Druse political group is the Progressive Socialist party, led by Walid Jumblatt, whose father, Kamal, was assassinated in 1977 by Syrian agents. The Druse now have close ties to Syria, where there is a large Druse community. The Syrians have supplied the Druse with a large assortment of weapons, including artillery and tanks. The Druse militia numbers about 4,000 men and has joined forces with the Shiite militia in and around West Beirut to battle the Christian-dominated Lebanese army and the Christian militias.

Another major Moslem force in the country—and a constant threat to it—are the 500,000 Palestinian refugees and the remnants of the Palestine Liberation Organization. The PLO leader, Yasir Arafat, and thousands of his troops were forced out of Beirut by the Israelis in 1982 and out of Tripoli by Syrian-backed PLO dissidents in 1983. The dissident PLO forces no longer recognize Arafat as their leader because of his lack of militancy in the fight with Israel. The Syrians, in addition to controlling these dissident members of the PLO, also control the 3,500-man Palestine Liberation Army.

This dependency on Syria by the Palestinian guerrillas, the Shiites, and the Druse has given Syria the major voice in the future political direction of Lebanon.

The Christians, who in 1932 made up a majority of the Lebanese population, are now only about 44 percent of the population. The largest Christian sect—and thus far the dominant one in the nation's political and economic life—are the Maronites. They number about 580,000 and make up 38 percent of the Christian population and 17 percent of the national population.

The Phalange party, headed by Pierre Gemayel, is the most important Maronite political group. Pierre Gemayel's son Bashir was elected president of Lebanon in 1983 by the nation's Parliament, but he was assassinated before he could take office. Bashir's brother, Amin, was then elected president, and it is his regime that the Syrian-backed Shiites and Druse have been trying to oust or to get to share political power.

The Phalangist militia is the largest of the Christian militias. It controls East Beirut, the area along the coast just north of the capital, and some areas in southern and central Lebanon. This militia has been heavily armed by the Israelis.

The Maronites have frequently fought among themselves. Suleiman Franjieh, leader of the Maronites in northern Lebanon, has long feuded with the Gemayel family and the Phalangists, who were accused of assassinating Franjieh's son in 1978. Franjieh, in fact, is pro-Syrian and has, at least temporarily, allied himself with the Sunnis of northern Lebanon.

Each of these peoples has played an important role in Lebanese history. Moslems and Christians have lived in harmony for long periods of time, but they have frequently engaged in bitter warfare, much as we are seeing today. To gain a better understanding of Lebanon's present conflicts, let us look back into the history of this war-torn land.

CHAPTER 3

A HISTORY OF CONQUEST AND CONFLICT

The first people to live in what is now Lebanon were the Canaanites, who are mentioned in the Old Testament. The Canaanites migrated to the area from the Arabian Peninsula around 3500 B.C. In time they came to be called Phoenicians, and they built a unique civilization on the eastern shores of the Mediterranean, in the coastal areas that make up modern-day Lebanon, Syria, and Israel. Not only did the Phoenicians develop an alphabet on which all future Western alphabets would be based, but they were the first people to base their economy on trade rather than agriculture. The Phoenicians were traders and explorers. At the height of their civilization they had colonies throughout the Mediterranean region, and it is possible that some Phoenician sailors made their way through the Strait of Gibraltar, sailing as far north as England and as far south as the southern tip of Africa.

With the decline of Phoenicia in the ninth century B.C., the area was ruled by a succession of conquerors. The first of these were the Assyrians who, in 842 B.C., captured the Phoenician coastal cities. The Assyrians were followed by the Babylonians, Persians, and Macedonians under Alexander the Great. Alexander's successors, the Seleucids, ruled Phoenicia until 64 B.C., when the Roman general Pompey conquered the area and made it a Roman province. It was under Roman rule that Christianity was introduced into Lebanon. During this period, too, the people of Lebanon, who had previously lived on the coastal plain, began to settle inland, in the mountains and in the Bekaa Valley.

Roman rule brought a long period of peace for Lebanon. A school of Roman law was founded in Beirut, and the city became an important base for the Roman fleet. Trade increased substantially, and Lebanon—where Western and Eastern ideas met and mixed—enjoyed a time of prosperity and cultural enlightenment.

During the second and third centuries A.D., many people in Phoenicia and other parts of the Roman Empire converted to Christianity, but they were cruelly persecuted by the Romans. It was not until 313 that Constantine the Great, the Roman emperor, declared in the Edict of Milan that Christianity was a legal religion in the Roman Empire. As a result of this edict, Christianity entered a period of rapid growth. By the time it became the state religion of the Roman Empire in 392, Christianity was already firmly entrenched in Lebanon.

In 395 the Roman Empire split into two parts: the Western Roman Empire, which was ruled from Rome, and the Eastern Roman Empire, or Byzantine Empire, which was ruled from the city of Constantinople. From this time forward, Lebanon was part of the Byzantine Empire, but the people of Lebanon did not support the Orthodox Christianity of the Byzantine rulers. Rather, their beliefs were closest to the beliefs of the rulers in Rome. This religious schism between the people of Lebanon and their Byzantine rulers would help bring about the fall of the Byzantine Empire in Phoenicia. But there were other factors as well, including high taxes and the harsh treatment meted out by the Byzantine governors.

In the 630s Arab invaders from the Arabian Peninsula swept across Phoenicia. They brought with them their new religion—Islam—and they called themselves Moslems: those who submit to God. Mohammed, the founder and prophet of Islam, had begun preaching his religion in the Arabian city of Mecca in 610. By the time of his death in 632, Islam had spread across the Arabian Peninsula. By 640, Moslem warriors had conquered Phoenicia. And within a hundred years, the Arabs ruled an Islamic empire that stretched from Spain in the west to India in the east.

When the Moslems conquered Lebanon, many of the people there welcomed them, for they were disenchanted with Byzantine rule. For this reason, and because the Moslems were tolerant at this time of other religions, the Arabs allowed the Christians and other non-Moslems to follow their own religious beliefs. The Moslems even used Christian officials to administer the lands for them.

This practice, however, did not last for very long. In the 660s the Moslems, who had moved their capital to Damascus in Syria, began to force the people of Lebanon and Syria to accept Islam as well as the Arabic language. Christian resistance to this was strong. The Maronite Christians, who lived in northern Syria, fled their homeland and established new villages in the rugged mountains of Lebanon. They were safe here for a while, but in 750 Moslem soldiers invaded the mountain strongholds, burning villages and destroying churches that had been built since the time of Mohammed.

Persecution of Christians was not limited to Lebanon. The Christians of Palestine were generally treated as second-class citizens, and their lot worsened when the Seljuk Turks took control of the Holy Land in the eleventh century; there were even some massacres. Jerusalem, then as now, was a city sacred to Moslems, Jews, and Christians. It had been under Moslem control since 638—a period of 450 years. Now, in 1095, Pope Urban II called for the ouster of the Moslems from Jerusalem and the Holy Land. The Byzantine Empire also wanted this, for the Seljuk Turks were bent on destroying it.

Beginning in 1097, a succession of Crusader armies left Europe to do battle with the Moslems. Initially they were successful. Jerusalem was captured in 1099 and, on the Lebanese coast, Tripoli fell in 1109. It was captured by the Frenchman Raymond de Saint-Gilles, count of Toulouse, who built a castle, Sanjeel, around which the modern city of Tripoli grew. Beirut and Sidon were captured in 1110 and Tyre in 1124. Soon, the Crusaders controlled the entire Lebanese coast as well as the Lebanon Mountains.

But European control of the Middle East would last for less than two hundred years. In 1144, the Moslems began their counterattack, and in 1187 Saladin, the great Egyptian warrior, took Jerusalem as well as many ports along the Mediterranean coast. Only Tripoli and Tyre remained in the hands of the Crusaders. In the late 1200s, the Mamluks of Egypt drove the last of the Crusaders out of the Middle East.

For Europe, the Crusades accomplished little. But they meant a great deal to the Christians of Lebanon, especially the Maronite Christians. Thousands of Maronites fought alongside the Crusaders, especially the French, and the Maronite religious leaders opened a dialogue with the Roman Catholic church. This was the beginning of the French-Maronite relationship that lasts to this day. The Crusades also initiated a period of strong commercial ties between Lebanon and Europe. But the Maronites paid for this. With the last of the Crusaders out of Lebanon, the Moslems slaughtered thousands of Christians and destroyed their villages in the mountains near Beirut.

The next tide to sweep over Lebanon was the Ottoman Turks, who were Moslems but not Arabs. The Ottomans defeated the Egyptian Mamluks, and conquered Lebanon along with neighboring Syria and Palestine in 1516. They would rule these lands for four centuries. At its peak, the Ottoman Empire included most of southwest Asia, all of North Africa except Morocco, and parts of southeastern Europe. Its capital was at Constantinople, the former capital of the Byzantine Empire, which the Turks had conquered in 1453.

The modern Lebanese system of sharing political power on the basis of religious affiliation was actually born when Lebanon was part of the Ottoman Empire. In the early 1500s, the Turks set up the millet system in Lebanon. Each millet, or religious community, was allowed to retain a certain amount of autonomy so long as it paid taxes to the Ottoman rulers. This system became fully entrenched by the sixteenth century. At that time, the Sunni Moslems controlled the area around Mount Hermon; the Kurds, a Moslem people who no longer live in Lebanon in substantial numbers, controlled Tripoli and the surrounding area; the Maronites controlled Kesrouan in central Lebanon; and the Druse controlled the area south of Kesrouan. The sectarian leaders were, of course, responsible to the Ottoman rulers, but the masses of the people then, as now, gave their allegiance to their local leaders, not to a central government.

It was during this same period, in the sixteenth century, that the Druse became an important force in Lebanon, despite the fact that they represented less than 10 percent of the population. Fakhr al-Din I, a Druse leader, had rallied his people to help the Ottomans drive the Egyptian Mamluks out of Lebanon. For this, the Ottomans gave him control of the Shuf Mountains between Beirut and Sidon. Today the Druse are still the dominant force in this area. Fakhr al-Din's grandson, Fakhr al-Din II, expanded the Druse-controlled area to include Tripoli, Baalbek, and much of the Bekaa Valley. He even ruled some parts of Syria and Palestine. Fakhr al-Din II was a masterful military leader and—when necessary—he would use his fierce warriors to subdue enemies. But he was also an incisive politician. He sought good relations with other religious sects and even forged an alliance with the Maronites. He permitted Christian missionaries to come to Lebanon, and he appointed a Maronite bishop as his representative in Rome and Florence.

Fakhr al-Din II became so powerful that even the Ottomans treated him as an independent ruler. He acted like one, too, making diplomatic agreements with European states and, in the process, building Lebanon into a prosperous trading center by exporting cotton and silk to Europe. His successes eventually became too much for the Ottomans to accept. In 1635 the sultan had him killed. Fakhr al-Din's successors continued to maintain relations with Europe, but none of them ever became as important as he was. Druse power waned because of internal strife, paving the way for the growing influence of the Maronite Christians.

As we have seen, the Maronites had established ties with Europe, especially France, during the Crusades. These ties were strengthened during the 1600s and 1700s. The Roman Catholic church set up schools in Rome to educate young Lebanese Christians, and the French founded schools and missions in Lebanon. Despite the fact that Lebanon was part of the Ottoman Empire, the French king, Louis XIV, claimed the right to protect Catholic subjects of the Ottomans. And in 1649 he stated that the Maronites were "in our protection and special safeguard." In the years that followed, the French opened consulates in Beirut and Sidon. Trade between the two countries grew. And the Maronites sent many young scholars to be educated in Europe. As a result, Lebanon became the only country in the Middle East to develop strong connections with the West.

During the 1700s and 1800s, the Maronites increased their strength and power in Lebanon by establishing close relations with other Christian sects, such as the Greek, Syrian, and Armenian churches. These people were permitted to settle in Maronite-dominated areas. American Protestant missionaries were also permitted to settle there, as were the Druse. But the Maronite leaders feared the Druse, and they frequently played off one Druse faction against another to maintain Maronite power.

During the early 1800s, Egypt was part of the Ottoman Empire, but it was largely independent, and twice in the 1830s the Ottoman viceroys of Egypt even fought against the Ottoman Empire. The Egyptians occupied Lebanon in 1832 and ruled it for ten years. Under Egyptian rule, Beirut became an important city, as trade with parts of Europe, especially France, boomed. Western influence became even stronger during this period.

Because the Christians dominated the trade with Europe—a trade that was beneficial to Egypt—the Egyptians gave them special concessions, an act that angered the Moslems. The Egyptians also permitted Protestant missionaries into Lebanon, and this was fiercely resisted by the Maronites. The Druse disliked just about everything the Egyptians did. As a result, by 1840 Lebanon was in a state of rebellion against Egyptian rule. The country's four major sects—the Maronites, Shiites, Sunnis, and Druse—united behind a Maronite military leader to fight the Egyptians.

At the same time, however, Britain and Austria joined forces with the Ottoman Empire to drive the Egyptians out of Lebanon and Syria. In 1840, British warships bombarded Beirut as Turkish troops landed on the coast. Ottoman rule was soon restored, but peace was not. For the next twenty years, Lebanon was wracked by bitter internal strife. The brief unity of the sects that had resulted from their common dislike for Egyptian rule quickly evaporated.

The major conflict developed between the Maronites and the Druse, as increasing numbers of Maronites moved into the Druse-controlled Shuf Mountains. The intense Druse resentment led to the massacre of 1860, in which Druse warriors in Lebanon, as well as in Damascus, Syria, attacked Maronite communities and killed 10,000 Christians. The nations of Europe rushed to aid their fellow Christians. France, supported by Britain, Austria, Prussia, and Russia, landed troops at Beirut, but by this time the Ottomans had already ended the slaughter—a slaughter that they, the Ottomans, had in fact instigated. Ottoman troops had even fired on Christians trying to flee the Druse assault.

Under pressure from the European powers, the Ottomans divided Lebanon into two areas: the first, which comprised the coast and the Bekaa Valley, had a Moslem majority; the second, Mount Lebanon (the Lebanon Mountains), now had a Christian majority. The various sects that lived in the Maronite-dominated Mount Lebanon—Sunni, Shiite, Druse, Greek Catholic, and Greek Orthodox—were represented on a council that advised the governor of the area. The governor, appointed by the Ottomans, was a non-Lebanese Christian who, it was hoped, would act impartially in disputes between the various sects. This system was a natural extension of the millet system and the forerunner of modern Lebanon's confessional system, which was formalized in the 1943 National Pact.

Mount Lebanon soon became a governmental and commercial model for the rest of the Ottoman Empire. By the end of the nineteenth century, Lebanon was prosperous. It had an outstanding school system. Beirut was the publishing center of the Middle East. And, through the Maronites, Western ideas became firmly established.

The Ottoman Empire had been in a state of decline since the late 1500s. During the 1800s, it lost most of its European lands to Austria and Russia—and to the newly independent countries of Greece, Serbia, Bulgaria, Albania, and Rumania. This steady loss of power and lands led to a revolt against the sultan in 1908 by a group of young army officers called Young Turks. At first, they wanted to introduce political and social reforms to the remaining lands of the Ottoman Empire, which consisted now of Turkey and parts of the Middle East, including Lebanon and Syria. But for a number of reasons the Young Turks became ultranationalistic. Lebanese and Syrian officials were ousted from the Ottoman government. The Turkish language—rather than Arabic—was used by Ottoman governors in Lebanon, Syria, and other Arab parts of the empire.

This Turkish nationalism led to a growth of Arab nationalism in Lebanon, where there were many who now sought either autonomy within the empire or complete independence. The Druse and Shiites, for the most part, preferred to be independent, primarily because Turkey was predominantly a Sunni Moslem state, and they feared that the Sunnis of Lebanon would eventually dominate them. The Maronites also favored independence, but other Christian sects were hopeful that Lebanon would become part of an independent Syria, where there was a strong Christian minority. They were joined in this hope by a large segment of the Sunni population, although some Sunnis preferred that Lebanon remain a part of the Ottoman Empire.

The downfall of the Ottoman Empire, however, was soon to take place. During World War I, the Turks allied themselves with the Central Powers—Germany, Austria-Hungary and Bulgaria—and their defeat spelled the end of the Ottoman Empire. French troops occupied Lebanon and Syria in 1918 and, beginning in 1920, ruled the area as a League of Nations mandate. Under the mandate the French were supposed to administer Greater Syria, which included Lebanon, until it was able to become an independent state.

But the French had other ideas and immediately separated Lebanon from Syria, enlarging what had been Mount Lebanon—the predominantly Christian area—to include the coastal cities, the Bekaa Valley, and other areas. The borders of present-day Lebanon were set at this time. But the Maronites, who strongly approved of the French mandate and who formed a substantial majority of the population in Mount Lebanon, now found that they formed only a bare majority in the newly enlarged Lebanon.

According to the League of Nations mandate, France was supposed to prepare Lebanon for independence in 1941. But in that year World War II was raging in the Middle East, and France did not really want to give up Lebanon. Independence finally came in 1943, although French troops did not leave until 1946. The 1943 parliamentary elections were won by Bishara al-Khuri, a Maronite, who became Lebanon's first president. He appointed Riad as-Solh, a Sunni, as prime minister.

The two of them formulated the National Pact, which allocated political power within the country to the various sects and set the tone of Lebanon's future relations with the West, and with the Arab states (see Chapter 1). With a seemingly workable accommodation between the nation's diverse groups, and with independence day coming on November 22, 1943, the Lebanese people set their sights on what they hoped would be a prosperous future.

CHAPTER 4

FROM INDEPENDENCE
TO CIVIL WAR

With independence, Lebanon entered into a period of unprec-
edented prosperity. The Lebanese people came to think of
their country as the Switzerland of the Middle East and their
capital city, Beirut, as the Paris of the Mediterranean. Commerce was their main concern, and they welcomed everyone
who had money to invest.

Wealthy Egyptians, fleeing from Nasser's rule, brought
their millions to Beirut. They were soon joined by Arab businessmen and Persian Gulf princes with millions in oil money.
The Lebanese banking industry boomed, and Beirut soon
became the financial capital of the Middle East, as well as the
major trading center for commodities and gold. With its repu-
tation established, Beirut saw an influx of British and American companies.

As the influx of money continued, the banks lent money to
local entrepreneurs to open businesses and factories. Office
buildings, luxury hotels, and high-rise apartment buildings
were erected—many of them overlooking the beautiful Mediterranean shore. This, in turn, attracted even more capital—
and it also attracted tourists.

Beirut quickly became the favorite vacation spot of wealthy Arabs seeking to escape the restrictive atmosphere of their own countries. The city's glittering night life attracted wealthy Europeans as well—as did the excellent skiing in the Lebanon Mountains and the white sand beaches along the Mediterranean coast. By 1971 tourism accounted for 15 percent of the nation's gross national product, bringing some $300 million into the country. And by 1973 nearly 2 million tourists were entering the country each year.

Tourism, along with other services and trade such as banking, finance, and commerce, now accounted for nearly 70 percent of the nation's gross domestic product. Industry, agriculture, and construction accounted for only 30 percent, but industry was growing at an annual rate of about 8 percent. However, the emphasis was on light industry, such as textiles, chemicals, and plastics; but in addition the country had built two oil refineries.

Lebanon itself has no oil, and it has few mineral resources. The scarcity of good arable land means that it must import much of its food. And, as mentioned above, it has no strong industrial base. Yet during its early years of independence it not only survived, it prospered. This was done by attracting investment from overseas. And this was accomplished only because the Lebanese provided foreign investors with a secure atmosphere that was conducive to good business.

The first signs that all was not so serene and relaxed appeared in the 1950s, not only because of internal problems, but because the East-West cold war had come to the Middle East and the Arab-Israeli conflict constantly threatened to spill over into Lebanon. The first Arab-Israeli War, in 1948, had resulted in the influx of hundreds of thousands of Palestinian refugees. The Christians of Lebanon feared that they could lose their preeminent position if the voices of these predominantly Moslem refugees were added to those of Lebanon's Moslem groups.

Camille Chamoun, a Maronite, assumed the presidency in 1952. He soon sought to strengthen Lebanon's ties with the

West, especially the United States. In 1955, Lebanon joined the U.S.-sponsored Baghdad Pact (from which it would later withdraw), and just a year later Gamal Abdel Nasser was espousing an anti-Western and Pan-Arab philosophy that appealed to a majority of the Moslems in Lebanon. Nasser's Pan-Arabism—a call for political unity of the Arab states— clearly frightened the Lebanese Christians, who did not want their country to become a part of a monolithic Moslem state.

The schism between Christians and Moslems widened in 1956, when Nasser nationalized the Suez Canal. This action precipitated a British-French military attempt to take over the canal, and was accompanied by an Israeli invasion of the Sinai Peninsula. This crisis quickly developed into a major East-West confrontation. The Soviet Union threatened to send "volunteers" into Egypt, and American forces around the world were put on alert. Every Arab country but one broke diplomatic relations with France and Great Britain. That country was Lebanon. The Lebanese Moslems, and some Christians, were outraged.

As the cold war deepened and the Soviet Union made greater inroads in the Middle East, President Eisenhower, in January 1957, put forth what is known as the Eisenhower Doctrine. It gave the president advance authority to stop Communist aggression in the Middle East. The congressional resolution that approved the doctrine stated: "The United States regards as vital to the national interest and world peace the preservation of the independence and integrity of the nations of the Middle East." The United States, it went on, would "use armed forces to assist any such nation or group of nations requesting assistance against armed aggression from any country controlled by international communism."

Chamoun was already hated by Lebanon's Moslems because he did not break relations with France and Britain after their attack on Egypt. Now, when he accepted the Eisenhower Doctrine, the idea of armed resistance to his government began to spread.

There were two events during the first half of 1958 that spread fear throughout the Christian populace. The first was the merger of Egypt and Syria into the United Arab Republic in February. The second was the violent overthrow of the Iraqi government, one of the most pro-Western governments in the Middle East.

The overthrow of the Iraqi government took place on July 14, at which time a revolt had been going on in Lebanon for two months. Chamoun's strong pro-Western position had already enraged the Moslems. In May 1958, he had tried to force Parliament to allow him to succeed himself as president—despite the fact that the constitution expressly forbade it. Chamoun's actions resulted in a revolt against his government. It soon turned into a Moslem-Christian civil war. The Moslems received some aid from Syria, which was being armed by the Soviet Union, so Chamoun called on the United States to honor its commitments under the Eisenhower Doctrine. On July 15, nearly 2,000 marines landed at Beirut. Within weeks, 12,000 more arrived.

The Lebanese Christians and Moslems soon resolved their differences—temporarily, at least. Chamoun agreed to give up the presidency, the fighting ended, and the American marines withdrew. Fuad Chehab, the Christian commander of the Lebanese army, became president. He had gained the admiration of the Moslems when, during the civil war, he had refused to obey orders to fire on the rebels. Chehab's foreign policy was less obviously pro-Western than Chamoun's; the Moslem-Christian differences were temporarily submerged, and the country returned to its pursuit of a prosperous economy. It was becoming clear, however, that only the Christians and a very few Moslems were benefiting from the growing economy.

Meanwhile, the hundreds of thousands of Palestinians living in Lebanon were becoming an increasingly important factor in the nation. The actions of the Palestinian guerrillas were threatening to involve Lebanon in the Arab-Israeli conflict that had been going on since the birth of Israel as a nation in 1948.

*The Druse leader Kamal Jumblatt
(in the center, wearing a dark suit)
was photographed with some of his
tribesmen in May 1958 at the start
of the Moslem-Christian civil war.*

Lebanon had not become involved in the Arab-Israeli wars that had been fought in 1948 and 1956. It had almost become involved in the Six-Day War of 1967, when Israel fought Egypt, Syria, and Jordan; but at that time the Christian commander of the Lebanese army refused to obey the Moslem prime minister's orders to assist the Syrians. To do so, he felt, would have meant the destruction of the Lebanese army.

While Lebanon was able to stay out of the major wars in the Middle East, it could not keep itself out of the conflict between Israel and the Palestinian guerrillas. The Palestinian refugee camps in Lebanon had become training bases for the guerrillas, and they conducted their operations from these camps against Israel proper and against Israeli interests in other countries. In 1968, for example, Palestinians attacked one Israeli airliner in Athens and then hijacked another Israeli plane over Italy. This last event brought Israeli retaliation: Israeli commandos attacked the Beirut airport and blew up thirteen airliners belonging to a number of Arab countries.

Fearing further Israeli retaliation, the Lebanese government began cracking down on the guerrillas. This led, in April 1969, to a confrontation between troops of the Lebanese army and Palestinian refugees, supported by Lebanese students. Shots were fired and a number of people were killed. After the government declared a state of emergency, the hostility of the Lebanese Moslems increased, and their demands that the government give the guerrillas a free hand were echoed by various other Arab governments. Warnings from the Phalangists that continued guerrilla raids would lead to an Israeli occupation of southern Lebanon fell on deaf ears.

In June 1969, as the guerrilla attacks continued, the Lebanese government demanded that the guerrillas leave the country. Unresponsive, the Palestinians stepped up their attacks until, in August, Israel sent fleets of planes to bomb and strafe Palestinian bases in southern Lebanon. Lebanon brought the issue to the United Nations Security Council, where the Israelis argued that the attacks were not against Lebanon, but against guerrillas who had murdered Israeli civilians.

The cycle of raids by the Palestinian guerrillas and reprisals by Israel continued. In May 1970, the Israelis invaded Lebanon, destroying Palestinian bases and capturing large quantities of weapons and ammunition. The Israeli forces stayed in Lebanon for more than a day. Two weeks later the guerrillas blew up a school bus in northern Israel. They killed eleven people, most of them children. The Israelis swept back into Lebanon again.

This time, the Israelis kept a large force inside the Lebanese border, and in fact controlled much of southern Lebanon until the end of July. Between the guerrilla attacks and the Israeli reprisal raids, life in southern Lebanon was totally disrupted.

In Jordan, meanwhile, Palestinian guerrillas were also conducting raids against Israel; these raids brought swift Israeli retaliation. The destructive Israeli raids and the Palestinian attempt to establish a state within a state in Jordan resulted in a confrontation with King Hussein and the Jordanian army, which, unlike the Lebanese army, was a well-trained and well-armed force. Within a week, the guerrillas were defeated. Their losses in Jordan, and in Lebanon from Israeli attacks, brought a temporary decrease in the level of guerrilla activity. The conflict between King Hussein and the Palestinians continued into 1971. In June a determined Hussein completely defeated the Palestinian forces. Thousands of guerrillas and civilians fled to Lebanon, swelling the ranks of the Palestinians already there.

Early in 1972, the Lebanese government and the Palestinian guerrillas reached an agreement that gave the government the right to veto planned guerrilla attacks that were likely to bring Israeli retaliation. But the guerrillas never fully cooperated with the government. During and after the Arab-Israeli war of October 1973, the guerrillas stepped up their raids on Israel, and once the Israelis defeated the combined forces of Egypt and Syria, they turned their attention to Lebanon. Almost daily, the Israelis pounded Palestinian bases and refugee camps. In May 1974, Israeli planes killed one hundred Palestinians and destroyed the Nabatieh refugee camp. These raids continued throughout the year, with Israeli planes striking closer and closer to Beirut. Commando bases on the southern fringe of the city were bombed in December. The first few months of 1975 saw no letup, and in May a number of Lebanese soldiers were killed in one attack.

Even as the Israeli-Palestinian war continued on Lebanese soil, Lebanon faced other problems. In May 1973 the army fought pitched battles with Palestinians. In May 1974, the Phalangist militia killed several hundred Palestinians in a series of battles. And in June, some Palestinian factions fought among themselves, leaving a number of dead. The violence continued into 1975. Students took control of the American University in Beirut and were forcibly ousted by the police. Shiite villagers in southern Lebanon were shot at by Lebanese army troops during a protest demonstration against Israeli raids. Strikes and a confrontation between the army and civilians over fishing rights left two dozen dead in Sidon.

The internal strife at this time was due primarily to the growing Moslem demands for a fair share of the nation's economic wealth and political power. The nation's economic growth in 1974 was 10 percent: industry was growing to such an extent that the government established a Ministry of Industry to promote and coordinate the growth. Yet the Moslem poor were living in inadequate housing. They had poor medical facilities. And whatever financial gains they had made were wiped out by the country's high inflation rate. With the constant Israeli raids, the fighting between the Lebanese army and the Palestinians and between the Rightists and the Palestinians, the economic deprivation of the Moslem majority, and the continuing hostility among the various religious sects, Lebanon, in early 1975, was truly ripe for a major conflagration.

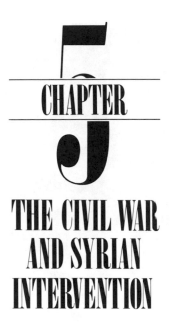

CHAPTER 5

THE CIVIL WAR AND SYRIAN INTERVENTION

The civil war that erupted in Lebanon in April 1975 was as complex as Lebanese society itself. It has been called a war between Moslems and Christians, but this is not a totally accurate description. A war between right-wing and left-wing forces is a more precise description. Certainly the right wing consisted primarily of Christians, but it also included Moslem groups that supported the government and that were strongly anti-Palestinian. Similarly, the left wing was heavily Moslem, but it also included Christians who had not benefited from the booming economy or who strongly opposed the Phalange, the Maronite Christian party headed by Pierre Gemayel.

The Phalange dominated the right wing of Lebanese politics; they were defenders of the status quo. They did not want to give up or share their political power or economic wealth with the Moslems or disadvantaged Christians. Because the Palestinians supported the Moslems in their quest for a more equitable distribution of power and wealth, the right-wing forces wanted the Palestinians out of Lebanon. The right wing

These leftist gunmen seek protection behind a sandbag barricade in the streets of Beirut during the 1975 war.

also feared that if the Moslems were given equality, the Christians' very independence and cultural existence would be threatened.

The Palestinians constituted the most potent force on the Left. Once they joined the fighting, their commandos accounted for 80 percent of the left-wing military strength. The various Palestinian groups frequently fought among themselves, but their greatest fear, and one that united them during the civil war, was that if the right wing defeated the predominantly Moslem forces of the Left, they, the Palestinians, would be attacked next. This was the primary motivation for the Palestinians involving themselves in the civil war.

Fighting side by side with the Palestinians were the Druse, the Shiite Amal militia, Socialists, Communists, and a variety of other groups including some whose loyalties were to Syria and Iraq. Each of these groups had its own militia.

The goals of the left wing were in direct conflict with the goals of the Right. They wanted a redistribution of the country's wealth and power, and they wanted the country—an Arab country—to pursue Arab nationalist goals.

The inability of the Right and the Left to reconcile their different needs led to one of the most destructive periods in Lebanese history. In a year and a half these contending forces practically destroyed their country.

The civil war began in April 1975 when a Phalangist was shot, presumably by a Palestinian. In retaliation, Phalangist militiamen ambushed a bus carrying Palestinian civilians through Beirut, killing 26 of them. In subsequent fighting over a period of four days, more than 150 people were killed. The Phalangists demanded that the government send the army against the Palestinians, but the Moslem prime minister refused to give the order. Phalangist members of the government condemned the prime minister. But Kamal Jumblatt, who was then the Druse leader and head of the Progressive Socialist party, blamed the violence on the Phalange. The entire dispute caused the government to fall. A new government, without the Phalangists or the Druse, was put together in the hopes of averting further fighting, but between late June and the end of August, nearly 1,000 people were killed in clashes between right-wing and left-wing militias.

In September, the fighting spread to Tripoli in the north. Dozens of Moslems and Christians were killed, including three Maronite priests. Looting was widespread and arsonists set fire to a number of buildings. The Lebanese army, which had Christian commanders, dispatched a force to Tripoli and joined the fighting against the Moslems.

In Beirut, Phalangist and Moslem militiamen escalated the fighting by using mortars and rockets. Stores were set ablaze. Mutilated bodies became a common sight on the streets. Soon every militia of every sect was involved. The Lebanese army—consisting of men from the various sects—disintegrated as the soldiers deserted to join their confessional militias.

"The orgy of violence," as one reporter described it, continued into 1976, with the Leftists gaining the upper hand. This was primarily because the Palestinians were now fully involved. West Beirut was soon taken from the Phalangists, and Beirut, for the first time in its history, became a divided city, and remains so to this day. Leftists also took control of Damour, south of Beirut. By March they controlled two-thirds of the country. The Christians controlled only East Beirut and the coastal area north to Tripoli, including the city of Juniye, the de facto Christian capital.

During 1975 and early 1976, Syria strongly supported the Palestinians and other Leftist forces. It gave them Soviet-made weapons and other military matériel. But when the Leftists seemed to be on the verge of complete victory, Syria became concerned that such a victory would lead to a pro-PLO Lebanese government, precipitating an Israeli invasion—and possibly an Israeli-Syrian war. Syria was not prepared for a war with Israel.

To forestall such a chain of events, Syrian President Hafez al-Hassad worked with Lebanese President Suleiman Franjieh to arrive at a compromise. The Syrian plan proposed that seats in Parliament be divided equally between Christians and Mos-

The Christian Phalangist party
erected this roadblock in Beirut
to warn pedestrians not to pass.

lems, and that Parliament, not the president, appoint the prime minister. The Syrian president believed that this redistribution of power would be acceptable to the Moslems, but the Leftists, now confident of military victory, rejected his plan.

On June 1—with the tacit approval of the Lebanese government, the United States, and Israel—Syria sent 30,000 troops into Lebanon. These troops, supported by hundreds of tanks, routed the Leftist forces in a matter of weeks. Syrian troops captured a number of PLO camps in southern Lebanon and supported Christian forces in their takeover of the Palestinian refugee camps near Beirut. The main Syrian thrust was aimed at defeating the PLO, and in this they were successful. In October, Yasir Arafat, the head of the PLO, met with the presidents of Lebanon, Syria, and Egypt and agreed to a ceasefire. It was also agreed that an Arab peacekeeping force, called the Arab Deterrent Force (ADF), would be established and that it would consist primarily of Syrian troops. For a time, the Lebanese civil war was over, but Syria was in Lebanon to stay.

What were the short-term effects of the 1975–1976 civil war? For one thing, none of the major combatants achieved their goals. The Christians, who had to be saved by the Syrians, were unable to consolidate their power. The Moslems did not gain politically or economically. And the Palestinians lost much of the freedom that they had had to operate independently in Lebanon.

The results for the country as a whole were catastrophic: the Lebanese government had collapsed; more than 40,000 people were dead; and the economy was ruined. Property damage was estimated at $2.1 billion. Most of the luxury high-rise apartment buildings and hotels in Beirut were gutted ruins, and tourism, of course, had ended as an industry. Foreign businesses fled the country to set up elsewhere in the Middle East—and Lebanese who could afford it also fled. The gross domestic product, which had been $3.2 billion in 1974, tumbled to $1 billion in 1976. And in 1977, 300,000 people still had no jobs.

While Syrian troops consolidated their hold on the central and northern parts of the country, the Israelis sought to control southern Lebanon, where the civil war never ended. Here Palestinians, many of them forced out of the Beirut area by the Syrians, continued to fight alongside the Leftists against Christian militias. The Palestinians were also opposed by the Shiites, the largest Moslem group in the area, who blamed the Palestinians for the destruction that had taken place in their region. More than a quarter of a million Shiites were forced to flee because of the constant artillery duels between the Christians and the Palestinians. Beginning in 1976, the Israelis armed the Christian militias in the south and gave them artillery support in their battles with the Palestinians. They also set up a "Red Line" along the Litani River and told the Syrian government that if its troops came south of the line they would be attacked.

The PLO rocket attacks on northern Israeli cities became more frequent in late 1977, as did guerrilla attacks across the Lebanese border. After one rocket attack in November, Israeli planes bombed PLO training camps and refugee camps, killing about one hundred people. In March 1978, PLO guerrillas killed thirty people who were riding on a bus in northern Israel. Most of them were children. The Israeli response this time was to send a force of 25,000 troops into Lebanon, where they killed 250 guerrillas, as well as 1,000 Palestinian and Lebanese civilians. They destroyed a dozen villages that had given shelter to the guerrillas. Palestinians and Shiites by the tens of thousands fled farther north to escape the fighting.

Within a week of their attack, the Israeli forces controlled most of southern Lebanon. The issue was brought before the United Nations Security Council, which hastily established a 6,000-man peacekeeping force with soldiers from ten different countries. The force, called the United Nations Interim Force in Lebanon (UNIFIL), was positioned between the Israeli forces and the Palestinians.

The Israelis agreed to pull their troops out of Lebanon, which they did between mid-April and mid-June, but they turned the territory over to a Christian militia under the command of Major Saad Haddad, a Lebanese army officer and a staunch Rightist. His troops, armed and trained by the Israelis, refused to let the Lebanese army move into the area. Haddad controlled an area that was seven miles deep, in which there were 40,000 Christians and 60,000 Shiites.

Israel supported not only the Christians of the south but those who were in East Beirut and the area just north of the city. The Phalange party and other Christian groups formed an alliance called the National Front to administer the Christian areas in and around Beirut. The National Front organized its own police force, set up food cooperatives and medical clinics, organized public transportation and garbage removal, and set up its own radio station. The Christian militias—dominated by the militia of the Phalange party—were increased to about 25,000, with several hundred Israelis acting as advisers. The Moslem section of Beirut was in a state of anarchy, with killings, kidnappings, and robberies occurring daily. Garbage was uncollected, and many kinds of food were scarce.

With Israeli support, the Phalangists gained strength and confidence and attempted to extend their control into other areas, especially the mountains east and north of Beirut. Many Christians, especially the Phalangists and most especially the Gemayel family and their close supporters, began talking about two Lebanons—one Christian and one Moslem—united in a federation. This talk, and the Phalangist domination of the other Christian sects, led to a split in the Christian ranks. Suleiman Franjieh was also a Maronite, but he was strongly pro-Syrian and he resented the Phalangist relationship with Israel. Franjieh not only opposed the partition of Lebanon into Christian and Moslem states, but wanted to work closely with the Moslems to build a strong unified state. Because of these beliefs, Franjieh formed an alliance with Rashid Karami, the Sunni Moslem leader of Tripoli, and the Druse. The infuriated Phalangists attacked the Franjieh's mountain home and killed Franjieh's son, daughter-in-law, and grandchild—as well as thirty of his followers. Franjieh's militia responded by killing twenty-two Phalangists.

The Syrian alliance with the Christians, the main purpose of which was to prevent a pro-Palestinian government from taking control of Lebanon, started to come apart even before the Israeli invasion in March 1978. In February, the Christian-dominated Lebanese army had fought pitched battles with Syrian troops, leaving 100 Syrians and 50 Lebanese dead. In April, the month after the Israeli invasion, the Syrians bombarded a Christian suburb of Beirut after Christian militias attacked Leftist militias. Now, in July, following the Phalangists' assassination of Franjieh's son, the Syrians unleashed a sustained bombardment of East Beirut, killing about two hundred Christians, most of them civilians. In August, the Syrians attacked Christian militiamen in northern Lebanon, and at the end of September they pounded East Beirut again. A United Nations call for a cease-fire and Israeli warnings that they would not allow the Christians to be massacred brought an end to the fighting.

During the first year of the 1975–1976 civil war, Syria supported Lebanon's Moslems and the Palestinians—a natural role for Syria. But when it seemed likely that a Moslem-Palestinian victory would force Israel to intervene, Syria switched sides and supported the Christians. Now, following the Israeli invasion of March 1978, the Syrians switched sides once again—this time to prevent an Israeli-backed Christian victory that could have led either to the partitioning of Lebanon or to the establishment of a pro-Israeli state.

For two years, 1979 and 1980, Lebanon experienced what can only be described as a period of "relative calm." There were still killings. There were still clashes between the militias. There were still PLO raids and Israeli retaliation. But for Lebanon, these were minor events compared to what had preceded them. The Phalangists continued to consolidate their control of the Lebanese right wing with Israeli military and economic support.

In the spring of 1981, however, when the Phalangists tried to extend their area of control, the Syrians resisted. There were clashes between Syrian troops and the Phalangist militia not only in Beirut, but in Zahle, a city in the mountains east of Beirut. Zahle is near the Beirut-Damascus highway and a gateway to the Bekaa Valley, which was controlled by the Syrians and PLO forces. When the Syrians threatened to overrun the Christian positions, Israeli jets joined the fray and shot down two Syrian helicopters. Syria responded by moving Soviet-built missiles into the Bekaa Valley, creating the possibility of Israeli air strikes and a frightening escalation of the conflict.

Meanwhile, the PLO continued its shelling of northern Israeli cities, and the Israelis seemed unable to stop them on the ground. As a result, on July 17, 1981, the Israelis took the war to West Beirut. Their intent was to destroy the PLO strongpoints, but they killed three hundred civilians in the process. A week later, the PLO and Israel agreed to a cease-fire. But for the remainder of 1981 and during the first months of 1982, tensions remained high. Despite the July cease-fire, the PLO, according to Israel, staged 130 attacks on Israel between July 1981 and April 1982. Also, in April 1982, the PLO assassinated an Israeli diplomat in Paris and killed an Israeli soldier on patrol in southern Lebanon. At this point Israeli troops crossed into Lebanon almost daily, searching for guerrillas, while the PLO responded by shelling Israeli settlements. On June 3 another Israeli diplomat, this one in London, was shot and critically wounded. The continuing war between Israel and the Lebanese-based Palestinians had reached a new level of violence.

CHAPTER 6

THE ISRAELI INVASION

On June 6, 1982, Israeli armored columns crossed the Lebanese border and smashed their way up the coast and into the southern Bekaa Valley. Continuing the push, thousands of Israeli troops—supported by jet fighters and naval ships—drove north to Beirut, where they trapped PLO leader Yasir Arafat and many thousands of his guerrilla fighters. What were Israel's goals in Lebanon? Defense Minister Ariel Sharon stated that Israel had "no intention whatsoever to keep any part . . . of Lebanese territory," and Prime Minister Menahem Begin declared that his sole goal was to drive the Palestinian forces out of southern Lebanon so that they would never again be able to attack settlements in northern Israel. This was a limited goal, yet here was Israel with one-fourth of Lebanon under its control. It would soon become clear that Israel not only wanted to drive the Palestinians out of southern Lebanon, but in addition wanted to destroy the PLO as a military force, ensure the installation of a pro-Israeli Lebanese government, and make Lebanon the second Arab nation to sign a treaty with Israel.

During their drive north to Beirut, the Israeli forces left a path of destruction in their wake. Palestinian refugee camps were hard hit, and the coastal cities of Tyre and Sidon—where the PLO had almost complete control—were extensively damaged. Tens of thousands of Palestinians fled north to escape the Israelis.

During their advance into the southern Bekaa Valley, the Israelis did not look for a confrontation with the Syrians. The Israelis had, in fact, sought to reassure the Syrian leadership that they did not seek a battle with Syrian soldiers in the Bekaa; but soon there were a number of clashes. Syrian jet fighters then took to the air to attack Israeli planes. Soviet-built ground-to-air missiles were also used against the Israelis. The Syrian-Israeli air battle had almost totally one-sided results: Israeli losses were minimal, but the Syrians lost eighty Soviet-built Migs and twenty SAM missile sites. The Israelis also destroyed the Syrians' radar command center.

By June 10 the Israelis were sitting astride the Beirut-Damascus highway. The forces that had raced up the coast completed their encirclement of Moslem-controlled West Beirut. With the highway to the east blocked, the 11,000 PLO guerrillas had no place to go. Israel demanded that they lay down their arms and leave Lebanon. To emphasize this demand the Israelis frequently halted the flow of all goods into West Beirut. For days at a time there was little food and few medical supplies; water and electricity were also cut off. When the Palestinians still refused to leave, the Israelis bombed and shelled the city. Hundreds of people were killed and wounded; apartment houses, shopping centers, and other structures were destroyed.

By late August it was clear to the PLO leadership that they could not remain in West Beirut. They finally accepted a withdrawal plan drafted by President Reagan's special envoy, Philip Habib, and agreed to by Syria and Israel. Under the terms of the agreement, the Palestinians turned their heavy weapons over to the Lebanese army. Then, between August 21 and September 1, the 11,000 guerrillas departed by sea for Syria, Iraq,

*Lebanese villagers greet Israeli soldiers
passing through their town in south Lebanon during
the 1982 war with the Palestinian guerrillas.*

*Palestinian guerrilla fighters fire their
guns in the air as they head for the ship that then
took them out of Lebanon in August 1982.*

Jordan, Algeria, and other Arab countries. Their evacuation was supervised by a multinational military force composed of U.S. Marines and troops from France and Italy.

The 800 marines stayed in Beirut for just over two weeks, returning to American naval ships just off the coast of Lebanon. They were kept there in readiness because President Reagan hoped that the evacuation of the PLO troops from Beirut was to be just the first step in the complete withdrawal of all foreign troops from Lebanon. But thousands of PLO guerrillas—as well as Israeli and Syrian soldiers—were still in the country.

Even as the PLO guerrillas were leaving Beirut, the Lebanese Parliament met to elect a new president. The individual they chose was Bashir Gemayel, the eldest son of Pierre Gemayel, leader of the Phalangist party. The 34-year-old Bashir had been the commander of the Phalangist militia. He was known as a ruthless fighter and was hated by the Palestinians, the Lebanese Moslems, and a substantial number of Lebanese Christians. As head of the Phalangist militia, he had been responsible for the murder of Suleiman Franjieh's family in 1978.

Gemayel was, in fact, the only candidate for the presidency. He had been a strong supporter of Israel, and many observers believe that he would not have been chosen if Israeli troops were not in the country and exerting strong pressure for the election of a "friendly" president. But in the days following his election, Gemayel sought to distance himself from the Israelis and adopt a more neutral position. He knew that he could not rule effectively without substantial Moslem support.

Gemayel's inauguration was scheduled for September 23, 1982. On September 14, as he was about to talk to hundreds of his supporters at the Phalangist party headquarters in East Beirut, a bomb exploded and Bashir Gemayel was killed. Almost immediately Israeli troops took control of West Beirut and the Palestinian refugee camps on the southern outskirts of the city. The Israelis called their move a "police action" that was meant to prevent a state of anarchy after Gemayel's death and stated that they would withdraw when the Lebanese army was capable of taking over and controlling the area.

At two of the refugee camps—Sabra and Shatila—the Israelis allowed the Phalangist militia to enter the grounds. The militiamen began killing men, women, and children— probably in retaliation for the assassination of Gemayel, even though there was no proof that Palestinians were responsible. They then used bulldozers to level parts of the camps and to bury and hide the bodies. It is estimated that the Phalangists killed more than six hundred Palestinians. The massacre was condemned by almost every nation in the world. Israel was blamed for allowing the Phalangists into the camps, and demands for the withdrawal of Israeli troops increased.

The Israelis did leave this Moslem section of the city on September 29, after turning control over to the Lebanese army. In addition, the multinational force of American, French, and Italian troops, augmented by British troops, returned to Beirut at the request of Amin Gemayel, Bashir's older brother, who, on September 21, had been elected to the presidency by the Lebanese Parliament.

When Amin Gemayel took office on September 23, his country was occupied by 30,000 Israeli troops, 70,000 Syrians, and 8,000 PLO guerrillas. Israel controlled all of Lebanon south of Beirut. The Syrians—and the PLO guerrillas under their control—occupied most of the Bekaa Valley north of the Beirut-Damascus highway and all of northern Lebanon including Tripoli. The Lebanese government controlled only Beirut and the corridor north to Juniye, the de facto Christian capital.

The Lebanese people had witnessed nearly eight years of warfare that had killed 75,000 of their fellow Lebanese and wounded 140,000 more. In 1982 alone, their country had been invaded by Israel, their president had been assassinated, and much of Beirut had been destroyed. Yet, amazingly, there was still some optimism at this time.

Amin Gemayel is a Maronite Christian and a Phalangist, but when he took office many Lebanese—Moslems as well as

Christians—believed that he would be willing to adopt a policy that could lead to reconciliation among the various religious sects. The stationing of the multinational peacekeeping force in Beirut added to the sense of optimism, and many Lebanese particularly welcomed the American presence.

Gemayel's first steps as president were generally applauded. In October he traveled to the United States to ask for economic aid in rebuilding Lebanon's shattered economy. He also asked for military aid to rebuild the army, so that the government could extend its control to a larger part of the country. And he asked the United States to help get the Syrian and Israeli troops out of Lebanon.

From this point on, the United States played an increasingly active role in Lebanese affairs. American policy in Lebanon had three major objectives: the first was to obtain the withdrawal of all foreign troops from the country—the Syrians, the Israelis, and the PLO guerrillas; the second was to help Amin Gemayel's government extend its control throughout the entire country; and the third goal was to obtain for Israel a secure northern border that would not be violated by Palestinian guerrillas.

While American diplomats—working closely with the Gemayel government and the Israeli government—toiled to find a formula for getting all foreign troops out of Lebanon and for securing Israel's northern border, the American marines began their task of rebuilding the Lebanese army, which had never recovered from the 1975–1976 civil war. Because the diplomats worked behind closed doors, the marines were the visible symbol of American efforts to put an end to the continuing tragedy in Lebanon. Their presence—they were deployed at the Beirut airport at the southern approach to the city—convinced many that the United States was committed to the support of the Gemayel government and that this commitment would be enough to end the strife.

The mood of wary optimism continued throughout the first half of 1983, but there were still violent incidents. The PLO Research Center in Beirut was blown up by a car-bomb in

February, killing eighteen people. In April the United States Embassy was destroyed by another car-bomb, killing sixty-three people. And in March, the American marines were attacked for the first time, though none were killed. But generally the level of violence was down, and the war-weary Lebanese people used the respite to assay the damage to their country and to begin the rebuilding process. Many of the country's roads were all but impassable. Sewer lines were ruptured, power lines were down, and hundreds of factories were in ruins. Nearly ten thousand homes and apartments were destroyed. Much of the destruction had been caused during the Israeli invasion, but some dated back to 1975. It was estimated that to rebuild all that had been destroyed would cost $18 billion.

As tentative plans were being made to revive the economy, Lebanese, Israeli, and American negotiators sought ways to get all foreign troops out of Lebanon. Philip Habib, President Reagan's special envoy, met with the Lebanese and Israelis for the first time in December 1982. Their meetings continued throughout the first three months of 1983, but in April Habib notified President Reagan that a number of points were holding up the completion of an agreement. In April, therefore, Reagan sent Secretary of State George Shultz to the Middle East to help with the unresolved issues.

On the way to Lebanon, Shultz visited Egypt, where he and Egyptian President Hosni Mubarak discussed Reagan's 1982 Middle East plan, which envisioned a Palestinian homeland affiliated with Jordan. From Egypt, Shultz traveled to Israel and then on to Beirut, arriving there on April 28. By May 6 Shultz was able to get an Israeli and Lebanese agreement to the withdrawal accord. Basically, the accord provided for the withdrawal of Israeli troops from Lebanon and for the establishment of a security zone in southern Lebanon, so that PLO guerrillas would not be able to attack northern Israeli settlements from Lebanese territory.

President Reagan called the agreement a "big step forward" that "can lead to the restoration of Lebanon's sovereignty throughout its territory while also insuring that southern Lebanon will not again become a base for hostile actions against Israel." But there were problems with the agreement right from the beginning. For one thing, Israel made its withdrawal contingent upon the simultaneous withdrawal of Syrian and PLO forces. President Gemayel was aware of the weakness of the agreement when he said, "The danger is, signing an agreement with Israel without obtaining the withdrawal of Syria . . . then Israel will refuse to withdraw. You will have a paper without any importance, any value."

Syria, indeed, had let it be known that it strongly opposed the Lebanese-Israeli agreement. And when Secretary of State Shultz flew to Damascus to try to win over Syrian President Hafez al-Assad, he came away disappointed. "It is fair to say," he commented, "that they [the Syrians] are hardly enthusiastic about the agreement." One Syrian leader called the pact an "act of submission" by Lebanon.

The agreement was formally signed on May 17, 1983. Because Article 1 of the treaty stipulated that "The parties confirm that the state of war between Lebanon and Israel has been terminated and no longer exists," Lebanon became only the second Arab nation ever to sign a peace treaty with Israel. Egypt had been the first. In 1979—under the sponsorship of American President Jimmy Carter—Egyptian President Anwar el-Sadat and Israeli Prime Minister Menahem Begin had signed a peace treaty after Israel agreed to withdraw from the Sinai Peninsula, the Gaza Strip, and the West Bank—Arab territories that Israel had captured during the Arab-Israeli wars.

For its efforts, Egypt was kicked out of the Arab League and ostracized by the Arab world. Syria now set out to punish Lebanon as well. It immediately blocked all roads leading from Lebanon to Syria and severed Lebanon's telephone links with the Arab world. In July 1983, Secretary of State Shultz met with Assad once again to try to persuade him to accept the Israeli-Lebanese agreement, but Assad told him that Syria's opposition was "final and irrevocable."

Syria's rejection of the accord came at a time of renewed

and intense fighting between the Lebanese army—which was being armed and trained by U.S. Marines—and Moslem militiamen. In the Shuf Mountains, where Druse and Christian villages nestled side by side, there were fierce artillery duels. The Israeli troops were often caught in the middle, and their casualties mounted. In the year between the June 1982 invasion of Lebanon and mid-1983, more than five hundred Israelis were killed and at least three thousand wounded—a very high casualty count for a nation of little more than 3 million people. Public opposition to the war was mounting in Israel, and a vociferous peace movement was demanding that the troops be brought home.

In an attempt to reduce their losses, the Israelis made plans to withdraw from the suburbs of Beirut and the Shuf Mountains. The plan was to redeploy the Israeli troops to positions along the Awali River north of Tyre. With a smaller area to defend, the Israelis would be able to send ten thousand of its troops back to Israel.

When Israel announced its intentions in July, the United States asked it to reconsider, because it feared that an Israeli withdrawal would precipitate renewed fighting between the Christians and Druse, each of whom sought to control the mountains. This is exactly what happened. The fighting between the Druse and the Christian militias and the Druse and the still-untested Lebanese army was fierce. Throughout the fall there were reports of massacres by both the Christians and the Druse.

The Shiites—like the Druse—were now being armed by the Syrians, and they were demanding that the Lebanese government scrap the May 17 agreement with Israel. The country was again faced with full-scale sectarian war. The optimism that had been felt at the beginning of the year was gone.

President Reagan's new Middle East special envoy, Robert McFarlane, tried to persuade Syria to reverse its stand on the Lebanese-Israeli troop-withdrawal agreement, but Assad once again refused to budge. He said that the agreement was "imposed on Lebanon" by the United States and Israel and demanded that it be disavowed, or else there would be no chance for a reconciliation of the various sects in Lebanon.

Meanwhile, the Druse were fiercely resisting attempts by the Lebanese army to take over strategic positions in the Shuf Mountains. The Druse also began firing at the American marines stationed at the Beirut airport, killing two of them on August 29. On September 6, two more marines, as well as a number of French soldiers, were killed, and both the United States and France began sending reconnaissance planes over Druse- and Syrian-held positions in the mountains and in the Bekaa Valley. Meanwhile, President Reagan ordered an increase in the size of the U.S. fleet off the Lebanese coast, and on September 13 gave the marines permission to call on naval planes and the navy's big guns for protection. The battleship *New Jersey* would soon arrive, and its guns could reach Syrian positions in the Bekaa Valley.

When President Reagan gave the marines permission to call on air and naval gun support if they were attacked, he also gave them permission to use this firepower to help the Lebanese army if its troops were in danger of being overrun by Druse militiamen in the Shuf Mountains. Naval guns were used to support the Lebanese army on a number of occasions, and it was at this point that the Druse and Shiite militias came to view the United States as a partisan in the war. The American marines had come as peacekeepers, but because of their defense of the Christians they were now viewed as enemies.

The fighting in the Shuf Mountains continued until the end of September, when a cease-fire was negotiated. The United States and Saudi Arabia played a major role in getting the Syrians to agree. The price for President Gemayel was the calling of a meeting with the leaders of Lebanon's major religious sects and political groups to discuss reconciliation. Plans were made to hold the meeting in Geneva, Switzerland.

A week before the meeting was held, a terrorist drove into the American marine headquarters compound at Beirut airport in a truck loaded with high explosives. The explosion destroyed the headquarters and killed nearly 250 marines. At the same time, terrorists destroyed the French military compound, killing 58 soldiers. The identity of the terrorists was never discovered, but it was thought that they had links to Iran—and that they could never have committed the acts without the approval of the Syrian government.

The deaths of so many marines created a furor in the United States. Questions had been raised about their role in Lebanon even before the first marine was killed on August 29, and a number of prominent Democrats and Republicans had demanded that they be brought back home. The 1973 War Powers Resolution restricted the use of American troops in hostile situations in foreign lands without congressional approval. The entire issue threatened to become a political football. But on September 29, less than a month before the marine headquarters was blown up, Congress authorized the president to keep the marines in Lebanon for another eighteen months, if necessary.

Even as more bodies were being pulled from the wreckage at the American marine compound, the Lebanese leaders were meeting in Geneva. Amin Gemayel represented the government, and his father, Pierre, along with Camille Chamoun, represented the Lebanese Front, a coalition of Maronite Christian groups from East Beirut and the mountains of northern Lebanon. Supporting Amin Gemayel were Saeb Salem and Adel Osseiran, who represented conservative, pro-government Sunni and Shiite groups. Aligned against Gemayel were Nabih Berri, the leader of the Shiite Amal organization and militia; Walid Jumblatt, the Druse leader; Rashid Karami, the Sunni

A U.S. Marine picks through the rubble in the aftermath of the bombing of the Marine headquarters at Beirut International Airport in October 1983.

leader; and the old enemy of the Gemayels, the Maronite Christian, Suleiman Franjieh. The latter three were members of the antigovernment, anti-Phalangist National Salvation Front.

These men, who represented most of the Lebanese people, met for five days, from October 31 to November 4. The members of the National Salvation Front as well as the other antigovernment leaders put a great deal of pressure on Gemayel to abrogate the May 17 agreement with Israel, but Gemayel refused. However, a compromise was agreed upon: Gemayel would not abrogate the agreement, nor would he ratify it. This was the only accomplishment—if it can be called that—of the five-day meeting of the most powerful men in Lebanon. They did agree, however, to meet again to discuss the overridingly important issue of more equitable power sharing by the various sects and political groups.

For the briefest moment, this gathering of Lebanon's political elite held out some hope for the future. But events through the end of 1983 and into the beginning of 1984 showed once again that the hatreds in Lebanon run so deep that a reconciliation of the nation's warring sects and the removal of Syrian, Israeli, and PLO forces from its territory would not come easily or in the near future.

Even as the Geneva meeting was getting under way, renewed fighting flared in Lebanon, this time between warring factions of the PLO. Yasir Arafat's ouster from Beirut by the Israelis in August 1982 had brought him condemnation by the more-militant members of the PLO. They accused him of being too soft. In this they were supported by Syria; the Syrian president had long despised Arafat and welcomed the opportunity to heap additional troubles upon him.

After leaving Beirut, Arafat had made his way back to Lebanon and set up a new headquarters in Tripoli. Near Tripoli were Palestinian refugee camps whose populations were Arafat supporters. The PLO dissidents challenged Arafat's leadership and then, with Syrian support, attacked the refugee camps and Tripoli itself. After heavy fighting, Arafat was forced to flee from Lebanon once again. This time he took with him only four thousand loyal troops. Clearly, Arafat was no longer the undisputed leader of the PLO.

Despite the September cease-fire agreement, fighting flared anew in December 1983 among the various militias. A more ominous note was the increased attacks against the multinational peacekeeping force by Druse and Shiite militiamen and Syrian attacks on unarmed American reconnaissance planes. The United States retaliated on December 4 by bombing Syrian antiaircraft batteries, but during one raid two American planes were shot down; one pilot was killed and his navigator, Lieutenant Robert Goodman, was captured. Within days, President Reagan reinforced the U.S. fleet. The year 1984 was about to begin with the Lebanese tragedy seemingly further from a solution than ever before.

CHAPTER 7

1984: LEBANON'S YEAR OF DECISION?

During the first week of January 1984, American civil-rights leader and Democratic presidential candidate Jesse Jackson traveled to Syria and, to the surprise and relief of everyone, obtained the release of Lieutenant Robert Goodman, the U.S. Navy navigator who had been shot down and captured by the Syrians on December 4, 1983. Syrian President Assad characterized his release of Goodman as a "humanitarian gesture." There were many who hoped that the Syrian gesture would lead to a dialogue between the United States and Syria, which would in turn lead to an end to the violence in Lebanon. Their hopes were soon dashed.

Even as Goodman was returning home, it was announced that Gemayel's government had reached an accord with the Druse and Shiites, and that government forces would be allowed to extend their control into those areas not occupied by Syrian and Israeli forces. But Walid Jumblatt, the Druse leader, kept putting stumbling blocks in the way. First he demanded clarification of minor points in the agreement. Then he demanded "a basic political solution" before disengaging his troops. By the end of January, it was clear that the Druse had no intention of allowing Lebanese government forces into Druse-held areas.

On February 2, the Lebanese army and Shiite militia battled in the southern suburbs of Beirut. As the fighting escalated, both sides started to use artillery and mortars and soon the fighting and shelling spread into East and West Beirut. Events now began to move so quickly that no one could predict their outcome.

Two days later Nabih Berri, the Shiite leader in West Beirut, called on the Moslem cabinet members in Gemayel's government to resign. He also told the Moslem soldiers in the Lebanese army not to fight against the Moslem militias. Within two days, Prime Minister Shafik al-Wazzan and the entire cabinet resigned. The United States urged Gemayel to form a new cabinet and to include Shiites and Druse, and Gemayel promised the Shiites and Druse that he would negotiate with them. But the fighting continued and more than seventy people were killed in two days.

With Gemayel and the Christians now standing alone in the government, and with the fighting escalating by the hour, increased numbers of Moslem soldiers began to desert the Lebanese army. Some just threw down their arms; others joined the Moslem militias. This was the beginning of the process that would shift the balance of power to the Moslems. The Israeli invasion in June 1982 had tipped the balance in favor of the Christians—especially the Maronites. Now the Syrians and their predominantly Moslem allies were gaining the upper hand, and they soon made their demands known: They wanted Gemayel to resign.

On February 6, in some of the worst fighting since the civil war of 1975–1976, the Moslems took control of all of West Beirut. Some of the troops that were still loyal to the government put up stiff resistance, but many more fled or joined the Moslem militias. During the fighting, rockets were fired at the U.S. Marine positions at the airport, and American planes and ships bombarded militia positions in the hills near Beirut.

As Gemayel saw his position weakening, he called on the members of the opposition to return to Switzerland for a new round of talks. Jumblatt and Berri refused to even discuss the matter. "No national unity can be established," Jumblatt said, "as long as Amin Gemayel remains president."

The Druse and Shiites consolidated their hold on West Beirut on February 7—the same day that President Reagan announced that he had ordered the marines out of Lebanon and onto the U.S. Navy ships in the Mediterranean. This change in course by Reagan was due to the steadily worsening political and military situation in Lebanon. Many congressional leaders applauded Reagan's decision because the stationing of the marines in Lebanon was becoming increasingly unpopular in the United States. But at the same time, the move was an admission that American policy in Lebanon had failed.

By this time the Lebanese army was falling apart. More than 10,000 of its 27,000 American-trained soldiers had deserted or gone over to the side of the Moslems, a situation reminiscent of the 1975-1976 civil war.

With the army falling apart, the Moslems and Druse pushed forward. The Druse drove army troops out of the hills overlooking Beirut and pursued them to Khalde, a town on the coast south of Beirut airport where the American marines were stationed. At Khalde, the Druse linked up with the Shiite militia, surrounding the marines. The remnants of the Lebanese army forces in the area fled south to the Israeli lines.

Gemayel appealed to his Syrian-backed opponents once again. He told them that if they would sit down and talk he would abrogate the May 1983 agreement with Israel. And, as part of an eight-part plan sponsored by Saudi Arabia, he also proposed a phased withdrawal of Syrian and Israeli troops; new talks leading to a sharing of power with the Druse and Shiites; discussions leading to changes in the structure of the government; the replacement of the multinational force by a United Nations peacekeeping force; and security arrangements for southern Lebanon, so that Palestinians would not be able to attack Israel from Lebanese territory. The plan was immediately denounced by the Syrians, Shiites, and Druse; they simply repeated their demand that Gemayel resign.

The Shiites, Druse, and Syrians were not the only ones calling for Gemayel's resignation. Many Christians now felt that Gemayel would have to resign. One former Christian cabinet minister stated that: "Either Amin Gemayel resigns and Moslems and Christians quickly agree on a successor, or else we are going to see another round of wide-scale fighting that will destroy what is left of the Lebanese system."

The Moslems had legitimate complaints about Gemayel. After the Israelis turned West Beirut over to the Lebanese army late in 1982, the army set about to disarm Moslem militiamen, but in East Beirut the army allowed Christian militiamen to keep their weapons. Gemayel also appointed Phalangists to every key post in the government. But—perhaps most important—Gemayel seemed unable to end the destruction caused by the civil war. The nation's economy was in ruins, and this affected the Christians as well as the Moslems.

The redeployment of the American marines onto the warships off the Lebanese coast was completed by February 26. On a number of occasions, these ships had bombarded Syrian and Druse positions, both to protect the marines as they were withdrawing and as a warning to Syria that the United States was not leaving Lebanon completely. But with the American marines out of his country, Gemayel had few options open to him. The option he chose was to go to Syria and confer with President Assad. It was clear that Gemayel's political survival was dependent upon his canceling the security agreement with Israel, despite Israeli warnings that they would stay indefinitely in Southern Lebanon if this happened.

In early March of 1984, Gemayel agreed to scrap the agreement with Israel, and the Druse and Shiites dropped their demands that he resign. Gemayel and his opponents once again traveled to Switzerland, where they held more unsuccessful talks on national reconciliation. It seemed clear that

Syria held the strongest hand and would dictate the terms of any possible settlement.

Syria did, indeed, force Gemayel to name the pro-Syrian Rashid Karami as prime minister. In April, Karami began the task of forming a government of national unity. The leaders of all the nation's sects were given cabinet posts. In addition, a special committee was set up to write a new constitution for the country—one that would give the Moslems a fair share of Lebanon's political power and economic wealth. Could this attempt to end the nine-year-long civil war succeed? Is there peace in Lebanon's future?

CHAPTER 8

THE UNCERTAIN FUTURE

Lebanon is at a crossroads. Israeli forces still occupy southern Lebanon, and the Syrians—now the dominant force in the country because of the withdrawal of the American marines—still occupy the northern and eastern sections of the country. It seems likely that Lebanon's two neighbors will maintain a presence in the war-ravaged country for some time to come. The reason for this is that Lebanon's problems are intimately entwined with the broader problem of finding a solution to the Palestinian problem and achieving a lasting peace in the Middle East. It is unlikely that the Palestinian people, who for nearly four decades have been attempting to establish a national homeland in Palestine, will attain their goal in the foreseeable future.

Israel has been in a state of war with the Arab nations and the Palestine Liberation Organization since its birth as a nation in 1948. It has emerged victorious from four wars with its Arab neighbors, but it has never won the peace. Israel has two goals: the first is to get the Arab nations to agree to live in peace; the second is to bring a halt to Palestinian raids on

Israel—raids that for the last decade have originated almost exclusively from Lebanon.

Under President Anwar el-Sadat, Egypt signed a peace treaty with Israel in 1979, but today Egypt seems to be reneging on its promise to normalize relations with Israel. The Lebanese signed what was in effect a peace treaty with Israel in 1983, but the Syrians, by supporting the Druse and Shiite opponents of the Christian-dominated government of Amin Gemayel, forced the abrogation of that treaty.

Today, Israel is almost back where it was prior to the signing of the peace treaty with Egypt. Perhaps it is in an even worse position.

Syria, which is armed and supported by the Soviet Union, is one of the hard-line Arab states that refuses even to accept the fact of Israel's existence. It supports those elements of the PLO that want to bring about an end to the state of Israel and establish an Arab-dominated secular state in all of Palestine— which includes what is now Israel, the Gaza Strip, and the West Bank.

This country, Syria, is today the dominant force in Lebanon. Since their entry into the Lebanese civil war in 1976, and most specifically since the Israeli invasion of June 1982 and the arrival of the multinational peacekeeping force—including the American marines—in 1983, the Syrians have played their cards like expert poker players.

They properly gauged American public opinion and, through the Druse and Shiites, applied military pressure in the right amounts and at the right times to force the withdrawal of the American marines. This effectively ended, at least for the present, American influence in Lebanon. Lebanese President Amin Gemayel struck a deal with Syrian President Hafez al-Assad because he had no place else to go.

Today, Israeli and Syrian troops face each other in Lebanon. Whether these two nations will go to war yet again remains to be seen, but it is certainly a possibility. What is certain is that Syria—with its newfound prestige in the Arab world—will make it even more difficult to achieve some kind of lasting peace in the Middle East.

This peace, of course, will not come until the Palestinian problem is solved. The Palestinian Arabs, some of them Christian but most Moslems, some of them living under Israeli rule in the West Bank, but most dispersed among the Arab nations of the Middle East, want their own nation, their own state. This deep-felt need and desire will not go away. Whether a Palestinian is working in the oil fields of Saudi Arabia or teaching in Egypt, what he or she wants most is a national homeland.

There are many moderate Palestinians who would accept a Palestinian state in the West Bank, but many others have devoted their lives to the destruction of Israel and the establishment of a Palestinian state in all of what was Palestine—before the United Nations partition plan became effective in 1948. Considering Israel's military strength, it seems unlikely that this nation can be destroyed.

Why then will Israel not agree to the establishment of an Arab homeland on the West Bank? For one thing, old hatreds die hard—especially in the Middle East. More importantly, the Israelis (and many Arabs) fear that a PLO-dominated Palestinian state in the West Bank would become a base for terrorists and a base for further Soviet penetration of the Middle East. The Soviet Union has long supported the PLO, as it has long supported Syria.

The Israelis, during their 1982 invasion of Lebanon, decimated the Syrian air force and destroyed many missile sites. But the Soviet Union has rebuilt the Syrian military establishment. Presently there are more than 7,000 Soviet military advisers with the Syrian armed forces—some of them at Syrian missile sites in Lebanon.

Despite the intransigence of Syria and other hard-line states such as Libya, Iran, and South Yemen, there are many moderates in the Arab world who would like an end to the fighting and destruction of the past forty years and a beginning to some kind of peaceful coexistence with Israel. These people know that the staggering expenditures of lives, money, and energy now used for the purpose of war, if redirected, could change the economic face of the Middle East.

The United States has been a strong supporter of Israel since 1948, but it has also been in the forefront of efforts to bring about a lasting peace. Today, despite American setbacks in Lebanon, the United States is working with such moderates as King Hussein of Jordan and President Hosni Mubarak of Egypt in an attempt to find a workable solution to the Palestinian problem. It is hoped that PLO chairman Yasir Arafat, after his defeat by Syrian-backed hard-liners in Tripoli in 1983, will join these moderates in their effort to establish a Palestinian "entity" in the West Bank, one that is associated with Jordan. It is feared, however, that Syria, with its new-found prestige and growing military might, will be able to intimidate Arafat, Jordan, and Egypt, and prevent any accord that would end the decades-old confrontation with Israel.

A resolution of the Palestinian problem would certainly make it easier for Lebanon to solve its problems, but it would not end these problems. The Lebanese people have a centuries-old history of sectarian violence. Will they now be able to subjugate their confessional loyalties and work for the good of the nation?

There are, no doubt, many Lebanese people who feel they are a part of the Lebanese nation. But their identity with the Lebanese nation continues to take a back seat to their identity with their religious sect, be it the Maronites, Shiites, Sunnis, or Druse. A decade of civil war has strengthened, not weakened, communal loyalties. And in Lebanon today there is fear and distrust of outsiders—meaning members of other sects. Lebanese society, always a mosaic of groups that worked—or was forced to work—together, has become fragmented. There are many who doubt that it can be put together again.

What are the possibilities for Lebanon's future? It is possible that the nation's political and confessional leaders will work out some compromise, that the Christians will share power with the Druse and Moslems, and that the Moslems will agree to harness the Palestinians so that their raids against Israel will cease and the Israelis will no longer feel compelled to occupy southern Lebanon. This is a possibility—but it is unlikely.

Another possibility is that Lebanon could be partitioned into Christian and Moslem states. If this happens—even if the Christian and Moslem states form some kind of federal union—Lebanon would be so weak that Israel and Syria would keep their troops there and dictate the fate of the nation.

A third possibility—one that would make an overall Middle East peace plan impossible to attain—is the annexation of parts of Lebanon by Syria and Israel. There are many Syrians who still consider Lebanon to be part of Greater Syria—the Syria that existed before Lebanon was separated from Syria during the early years of the French mandate. Similarly, there are many Israelis who claim that southern Lebanon was part of ancient Israel, and there are many more who would like Israel to have the water resources in that part of Lebanon. The ramifications of the partition of Lebanon would be impossible to predict, but war between Syria and Israel—each supported by a superpower—would not be an impossibility.

The history of Lebanon, most especially its recent bloody history, has been so full of twists and turns that the only safe expectation is that solutions to the nation's problems will not come easily.

FURTHER READING

Ayoob, Mohammed (ed.), *The Middle East in World Politics,* St. Martin's Press, 1981.

Dawisha, Adeed J., *Syria and the Lebanese Crisis,* St. Martin's Press, 1980.

Deeb, Marius, *The Lebanese Civil War,* Praeger, 1980.

Fisher, Sydney N., *The Middle East: A History,* Knopf, 1978.

Fuller, Anne H., *Buarij, Portrait of a Lebanese Muslim Village,* Harvard University Press, 1961.

Gabriel, Richard A., *Operation Peace for Galilee: The Israeli-PLO War in Lebanon,* Hill & Wang, 1984.

Gordon, David C., *Lebanon: The Fragmented Nation,* Hoover Institution Press, 1980.

Haley, P. Edward, and Snider, Lewis W. (eds.), *Lebanon in Crisis,* Syracuse University Press, 1979.

Peretz, Don, *The Middle East Today,* Holt, Rinehart & Winston, 1978.

Randal, Jonathan C., *Going All the Way: Christian Warlords, Israeli Adventurers, and the War in Lebanon,* Viking Press, 1983.

CHRONOLOGY

3500 B.C. to 9th century B.C.	Lebanon is part of Phoenicia, which also includes the coastal areas of Syria and Palestine.
9th to 6th century B.C.	Assyrian rule.
6th century B.C.	Babylonian rule.
6th to 4th century B.C.	Persian rule.
4th century B.C. to 64 B.C.	Macedonian and Seleucid rule.
64 B.C. to 395 A.D.	Part of the Roman Empire.
395 to 636	Part of the Byzantine Empire.

636 to 1099	Arab rule.
1099 to 1291	Ruled by the Crusaders.
1291 to 1516	Egyptian Mamluke rule.
1516 to 1918	Part of the Ottoman Empire.
1918 to 1943	Part of the French League of Nations Syria-Lebanon mandate.
1943	November 22: Lebanon becomes an independent country.
1948	Israel becomes an independent nation and hundreds of thousands of Palestinian refugees flee to Lebanon as a result of the first Arab-Israeli War.
1958	American marines are sent to Lebanon to help end a Moslem-Christian civil war.
1968	In retaliation for Palestinian guerrilla attacks against Israel and Israeli civilian planes, Israeli commandos attack Beirut airport and blow up thirteen Arab airliners.
1969	Palestinian attacks against Israel and Israeli retaliation against Palestinian bases in Lebanon increase in frequency.
1970–1971	Palestinian guerrillas ousted from Jordan arrive in Lebanon, making it the only Arab country from which raids are conducted against Israel. The Palestinians set up a "state within a state" in Lebanon.

1975–1976	April: The Lebanese civil war begins and soon involves Palestinian guerrillas as well as Christians and Moslems.
1976	Syrian troops enter the civil war and occupy substantial parts of northern and eastern Lebanon.
1978	March 14: Israel invades Lebanon.
	April 1: The U.N. Interim Force in Lebanon arrives in southern Lebanon and establishes a buffer zone between Israeli and PLO forces.
	June 13: Israelis withdraw from Lebanon after establishing a security zone along its northern border.
1981	April: Syria moves SAM missiles into Lebanon after the Israelis shoot down two Syrian helicopters.
1982	June 6: Israeli forces invade Lebanon. They reach Beirut in a few days and trap PLO forces in that city, demanding that they leave Beirut.
	August 21: The PLO begins its evacuation of Beirut, supervised by a multinational peace-keeping force consisting of U.S. Marines and troops from France and Italy.
	August 23: The Lebanese Parliament elects Bashir Gemayel, a Maronite Christian, president of Lebanon.

1982 (*continued*)	September 10: With the PLO evacuation completed, U.S. Marines and other members of the multinational peacekeeping force leave Beirut.
	September 14: Bashir Gemayel is assassinated.
	September 21: Amin Gemayel, brother of Bashir Gemayel, is elected president of Lebanon.
	September 29: Israeli forces leave West Beirut after handing it over to the Lebanese army. The multinational peacekeeping force, including 2,000 U.S. Marines, returns to Beirut to help the Lebanese army establish control.
1983	April 18: Sixty-three people are killed when terrorists blow up the U.S. embassy in Beirut with a car-bomb.
	May 17: Lebanon and Israel sign an agreement for the withdrawal of Israeli forces from Lebanon and for the establishment of a security zone in southern Lebanon to end PLO attacks against northern Israel, but Israel says that it will not withdraw until Syrian troops leave Lebanon.
	September 4: Because of increasing casualties, Israeli forces pull back to the Awali River, north of Sidon in southern Lebanon. Fighting erupts between Druse and Christian militias.

1983 *(continued)*	September 6: The Lebanese army joins the Christian militias against the Druse.
	September 17: U.S. naval ships pound Druse positions.
	September 25: A cease-fire is arranged and plans for a national reconciliation conference are made.
	October 23: Moslem fundamentalist terrorists, with links to Iran, kill nearly 250 American marines and 58 French soldiers in suicide-bomb attacks.
	October 31–November 4: President Gemayel and the leaders of the various sects meet in Geneva, Switzerland, to discuss national reconciliation.
	December 4: Syrian missiles down two U.S. Navy jets. One pilot is killed, and his navigator, Lieutenant Robert Goodman, is captured.
1984	January 3: U.S. civil-rights leader and Democratic presidential candidate Jesse Jackson obtains Goodman's release from Syria.
	February 2: Shiite militiamen and Lebanese army engage in fierce fighting in Beirut's southern suburbs.
	February 6: Moslem militiamen take West Beirut and the Lebanese army begins to disintegrate.

1984
(*continued*)

February 7: President Reagan announces that the U.S. Marines will be redeployed to U.S. Navy ships sitting off the coast of Lebanon.

March 5: President Gemayel abrogates agreement with Israel.

March 12: President Gemayel and the leaders of Lebanon's various political groups and religious sects meet in Lausanne, Switzerland, for reconciliation talks which end in failure.

April 26: Rashid Karami is named prime minister; he attempts to form a government of national unity.

INDEX